Looking for The Promise of The Blessed Hope

Why we still believe in the doctrine of the Rapture

By August Rosado

Today in Bible Prophecy Ministries

Contents

All Scripture in this book is taken from the King James Version

Visit us at

Www.todayinbibleprophecy.org

Invite August Rosado to speak at your church on Bible prophecy

Join August on a Bible Prophecy tour of Israel

Dedicated to my wife Patty Rosado who has stood by my side for 30 years

The Blessed Hope

The doctrine of the blessed hope is the theme that permeates the pages of holy Scripture. It is the promise that the believer could look forward to in terms of Jesus soon return. In a world that we live in today ravaged by sin and immorality at an all-time high, we as followers of Jesus can rest assure that He will call His bride home. When we read Titus 2:13, we see two phases of the second coming. The first phase is the blessed hope, the Rapture of the church, the second phase, is the second coming at the end of the 7-year tribulation period.

At the first phase we will meet Jesus in the air, at the second coming, we return with Him riding on white horses. In my last book, "Bible Eschatology", I look at the Geo-Political activities that are last days indicators that the end times are soon to come upon the world. I differentiate between the last days of the church age, and the end times of Daniel's 70th Week of prophecy. We are in the gap period between the 69th and the 70th week of prophecy as I will address in this book. The church is the gap of time. The church age, since its conception at Pentecost has paused God's prophetic time clock.

The 69 weeks of Daniel's prophecy was the heart beat during that specific period. When the 69 weeks ended, the heart beat flatlined. God paused the clock and we have been in that pause period, the gap period, the flat-line period if you will. One-day God will un-pause the button, the flatline will get a pulse, the heart beat will begin beating again. This heart beat will be the 70th week of Daniel's prophecy. The last days of the church age is about to end at the Rapture. The 70 weeks will commence sometime after the church has been taken out. All indicators are that those events are soon to commence, but not before the church has been removed by the Lord Jesus.

It is my prayer that this book will bless as well as challenge you in your walk with the Lord. To give you that yearning for Jesus soon return. Its unfortunate today that the church is yawning, rather than yearning for the Rapture. We are robbing our people of the doctrine of the blessed hope by failing to preach

Jesus soon return behind the pulpits of America today. We are no longer sharing the gospel, we have become desensitized by the sin of society today. False doctrine and heresy have permeated the church by and large. The Friends of Israel Gospel Ministry in their January 2018 issue of the magazine had the title, "Whatever Happened to The Doctrine of The Rapture?". The doctrine of the blessed hope is under attack.

The doctrine of the Pre-Tribulation Rapture is under attack. It seems like the church is beginning to lose hope that Jesus is coming back. On April 18, 2014 a Cardinal at the Vatican made the statement that the Catholic church will no longer wait for Jesus soon return. They said Jesus may not return after all, but that does not mean we are to give up the faith they said. This is in line with 2 Peter 3:3-4 where it says in the last days they would deny Jesus soon return,

3 Knowing this first, that there shall come in the last days scoffers, walking after their own lusts,

4 And saying, Where is the promise of his coming? for since the fathers fell asleep, all things continue as [they were] from the beginning of the creation.

This is the problem today with the 21st century church. The doctrine of the Rapture is being forsaken behind the pulpit. We are throwing out the baby with the bathwater. We need to preach this timely truth today to get evangelistic in sharing the gospel with a lost and dying world. Bible prophecy will motivate us to do just that! Therefore, Titus 2:13 tells us,

11 For the grace of God that bringeth salvation hath appeared to all men,

12 Teaching us that, denying ungodliness and worldly lusts, we should live soberly, righteously, and godly, in this present world;

13 Looking for that blessed hope, and the glorious appearing of the great God and our Savior Jesus Christ;

Bible prophecy motivates us to live godly in an age of ungodliness. To live spiritual in an age of worldly desires. Bible prophecy moves us to be a light to the world, (Matt 5:16). I pray that this book will help you and I to do just that.

Maranatha!

August

The Doctrine of Imminence Considering the Rapture
Revelation 22:20

"He which testifieth these things saith, Surely I come quickly. Amen. Even so, come, Lord Jesus."

The Doctrine of Imminence in the Bible is one of the clearest doctrines in Scripture in relation to the coming of Jesus for the church at the next main event on God's calendar of events, the Rapture. The doctrine of Imminence has been discussed and debated among believers as not to the timing of the Rapture, but, as to what, if any signs or prophecies precede the Rapture of the church.

The definition of the word "Imminence" simply means 'the state or fact of being about to happen'. An event that is about to happen without anything preceding the event. In other words, there is no heads up. If I was to put this in a sentence it would read this way: "the populace was largely unaware of the imminence of war". Notice the word, "unaware". There are no signs that precede the war, the population was unaware.

We see the doctrine of imminence replete in the New Testament about Jesus soon coming. To deny this truth is to deny the doctrine that Jesus could return without any pre-conditions. If we reject the doctrine of imminence, what we are saying, is that there must be signs that have to be fulfilled for Jesus to return. There are prophecies that must come to pass for the Rapture to happen.

According to Dr. Renald Showers, the doctrine of imminence would mean, "Hanging over one's head, ready to befall or overtake one, close at hand in its incidence. In other words, it will overtake a person without warning. There are things that may happen before the events, last day indicators that Jesus coming is close at hand, but there are no prophecies that must take place before the event occurs. If something else must happen before that event, then that event is not imminent."

If something else must happen before the Rapture of the church, then that destroys the concept of imminence. The necessity of an event that must be fulfilled eliminates the concept of imminence. When you have an event like the Rapture that is truly imminent, a person will never truly know when the Rapture will take place. He has no heads up as to when it will take place. He may see indicators Jesus is near, but, no major signs or prophecies having to be fulfilled.

A. T. Pierson stated, "Imminence is the combination of two conditions, certainty and uncertainty. By an imminent event we mean one which is certain to occur at some time, uncertain at what time. A person cannot legitimately set a date for an imminent event. When a date is set it destroys the concept of imminence. A set date is not only unscriptural but is contrary to the concept that an event can occur at any time.

When we read Revelation 22:20, Jesus in His own words tell us, *"Surely I come quickly"*. Jesus never attached any signs or prophecy that must come to pass before He returns for Hid Bride, the church. The final promise in the Bible to close out the cannon of Scripture, is the imminent return of the Lord.

The Bible opens with the promise of His first coming in Genesis 3:15, the Protoevangelium. The first advent of Jesus. The Scriptures close on the promise of His soon coming. When John the Apostle says, *"Even so come Lord Jesus"*, it is equivalent to the Aramaic expression Maranatha. Maranatha literally means, "Our Lord Come". It is an expression found in 1 Corinthians 16:22.

Maranatha was the first century greeting of the early church. They anticipated the Lord's soon return even in their day. They knew His coming was imminent. They hoped and prayed Jesus would come in their lifetime. The word "quickly", is the Greek word, *"Tachu"*, and is found 4 times in the book of Revelation. It refers to the imminent coming of the Lord. His coming with so signs attached to it, no prophecies preceding it.

We find in Revelation 3:11, "*I come quickly*". The imminent return of Jesus for his church at the Rapture.

We see in 22:7, "*I come quickly*", 22:12, "*I come quickly*", 22:20, "*I come quickly*". This all implies imminence. In Revelation 22:10 John tells us, "Seal not the sayings of the prophecy of this book: for the time is at hand". This shows His return is imminent. It is not an elongated period, but an action that can happen at any time, at any moment.

God told Daniel to seal his book, to seal it up, because these prophecies would not be fulfilled in Daniel's day, (Dan 12:4). We see in Daniel 12:9 that God reiterates again that Daniel's prophecies would be sealed until the time of the end. Now that Jesus has come, was crucified, buried, risen from the dead, ascended back into heaven, John was told not to seal his prophecies. Why? Because Jesus coming is now imminent. He can return anytime.

Paul the Apostle said in 1 Corinthians 7:29, "*brethren, the time is short:*" Paul anticipated the Lord to come in his day. The Apostle knew Jesus coming was imminent. Obviously, Jesus did not come in his day even though it was imminent. The Bible clearly displays the imminence of Jesus soon return. Revelation 3:11; 22:7; 22:12; 22:20. To deny this is to deny the clear teaching of Scripture. Nothing else must be fulfilled for the Rapture to take place. The promise of the Blessed Hope, as succinctly defined by Dr. Showers will one day befall us, overtake us, it is close at hand in its incidence, it could happen at any moment without any pre-conditions. We may see many last days indicators that we are approaching that time. 2 Timothy 3:1-5 is a last day indicator of the collapse of morality, 1 Timothy 4:1-3 is a last day indicator concerning predictions of Apostasy.

We have last day indicators that we are living in the Times and Seasons of the Lord's coming in 1 Thessalonians 5:1-3,

1 But of the times and the seasons, brethren, ye have no need that I write unto you.

2 For yourselves know perfectly that the day of the Lord so cometh as a thief in the night.

3 For when they shall say, Peace and safety; then sudden destruction cometh upon them, as travail upon a woman with child; and they shall not escape.

Times, is the Greek word *chronos*, it denotes "periods of times". Seasons is the Greek word *karios*, which are "specific points of times". We are living in a period of time in which the imminent coming of the Lord is near. However, no signs precede it. In the tribulation period, you have specific points of time, *karios*, because there are many signs that accompany Daniel's 70th Week of prophecy.

Jesus could return at any moment. Conditions for His appearing is ripe. We have last days indicators that the end times will soon come upon this world. His coming in imminent. The Rapture is the next event!

Notes

Who Are the Four & Twenty Elders?

Revelation 4:4

"And round about the throne were four and twenty seats: and upon the seats I saw four and twenty elders sitting, clothed in white raiment; and they had on their heads crowns of gold."

Revelation chapters 4-5 describe a scene in heaven of a group praising God as He is seated on His Throne in heaven. Daniel describes God as the Ancient of Days, (Dan 7:13). The group around the Throne of God that are praising God and worship Him are known as the "Four and Twenty Elders" or 24 Elders. There has been much debate as to these 24 Elders are.

John the Apostle sees 24 seats or thrones around God's Throne. Sitting on those seats are the 24 Elders. John describes them as wearing white remnant with crowns of gold on their heads. This should give us a clue as to the identity of these 24 elders. This group of 24 Elders are mention 7 times in the book of Revelation., (Rev 4:4; 10; 5:8; 11; 14; 7:11; 11:16). Whenever they are mentioned the scene is in heaven, not the earth.

I would say the evidence points to the 24 Elders being the church that was Raptured and taken to heaven by the Lord Jesus. I say this because of the description of this group wearing white apparel and dawning crowns on their heads. We see in Revelation 4:10 this same 24 Elders taken those crowns off their heads and casting them before the Throne of God, singing that God alone is worthy to receive glory, honor, and power.

Where did these crowns come from? How did this group of 24 Elders obtain those crowns? Well, no doubt from the judgment seat of Christ, (2 Cor 5:10; Rom 14:10; 12; 1 Cor 3:11-15). The Bible describes five crowns that believers can obtain in service to the Lord while on earth. The Bible describes:

A crown of Incorruption-1 Corinthians 9:25, for faithfully running the race

A crown of Life- James 1:12 & Revelation 2:10, for overcoming temptations and to suffer martyrdom

A crown of Rejoicing- 1 Thessalonians 2:19, for winning souls to the Lord

A crown of Glory- 1 Peter 5:2-4, For faithful Pastors who feed God's flock the Word of God A crown of Righteousness- 2 Timothy 4:7-8, those who long for Jesus soon return.

These crowns were probably distributed to these Elders at the Judgment Seat of Christ, or Bema Seat. The Christian is rewarded for faithful service by receiving these crowns. We see in heaven these crowns placed at the foot of God's Throne. The crowns in Revelation are in the Greek *Stephanos,* the crowns of rewards at the Bema Seat of Jesus. Those who worship the Lord place these crowns at His feet and exalt Him in worship by saying,

"Thou art worthy, O Lord, to receive glory and honour and power: for thou hast created all things, and for thy pleasure they are and were created."

The 24 Elders are clothed in white raiment. We see in Revelation 19:14 when Jesus returns at His second coming, the army following Him on white horses is also clothed in white raiment, this is the church coming back with him. All the evidence suggest that these 24 Elders are the church who are clothed in white raiment and received the *Stephanos,* the crowns at the Judgment Seat of Christ. They receive these rewards in heaven.

The number 24 represents the church as Priest before God. We see in the Old Testament that king David divided the Levitical Priesthood in 24 sections or divisions, (2 Chron 24:7-19). We see in Luke's gospel that Zechariah was of the course of Abijah, a division of 24 Priest doing service in the Temple at Jerusalem in Luke 1:5 and 8. This goes back to David in 2 Chronicles 24.

Whenever we see these Four and Twenty Elders in the book of Revelation, it is either before the tribulation, or during the parenthetical chapters in the book that give us additional information. A parenthetical chapter in the book of Revelation is like a break or a pause moment to give the reader a side note if you will. An example chapter is chapter 7 concerning the 144,000 Jews. When we get to verse 9-11, the scene shifts from earth to heaven concerning the numberless multitude,

9 After this I beheld, and, lo, a great multitude, which no man could number, of all nations, and kindreds, and people, and tongues, stood before the throne, and before the Lamb, clothed with white robes, and palms in their hands;

10 And cried with a loud voice, saying, Salvation to our God which sitteth upon the throne, and unto the Lamb.

11 And all the angels stood round about the throne, and [about] the elders and the four beasts, and fell before the throne on their faces, and worshipped God,

Another example is Revelation chapter 11 concerning the Two Witnesses on earth. The scene once again shifts from earth, where the Two Witnesses are to heaven in verse 16 where the 24 Elders worship God,

16 "And the four and twenty elders, which sat before God on their seats, fell upon their faces, and worshipped God,"

My point is, whenever you read about this 24 Elders group it is either before the tribulation or the scene is in heaven, not on the earth. This proves for a Pre-Tribulation doctrine in conjunction with other proof text. The 24 Elders are the Raptured church in heaven before the Throne of God and they cast their crowns at his feet and worship Him in praise and exaltation. They are clothed in white raiment and glorify God.

A recent Breaking Israel News report stated that Jews on the Temple Mount reacted to Arab anger and rage by Praising God at Judaism's holiest site, the site of both Jewish Temples in Jerusalem, the Temple Mount. One of them was Rabbi Yisreal Ariel, a respected Rabbi in Jerusalem who founded the Temple Institute with the goal of rebuilding the third Jewish Temple. He is a frequent visitor to the Temple Mount.

As the Muslim guards on the Temple Mount, or the Waqf, began to shout at the Jews, "Allahu Akbar", the Jews shouted back in Hebrew, "Adonai Hoo, Ha, Elohim", 'God is our Master'. Some Jews prayed the Shema od Deuteronomy 6:4. What a great way to confront anger or bitterness, just praise the Lord!

Pray it in Hebrew, "Hoah, Dah HaShem". That is how the Jews confronted Arab trouble makers on the Temple Mount, just praised the Lord! We need to do the same thing in the here and now, just praise the Lord in every situation. When we get to heaven, Revelation chapters 4-5 record a great Hallelujah session before God's Throne. I am convinced the 24 Elders is the church, the Saints that were Raptured before the Tribulation period.

Revelation records them around God's Throne in heaven in praise to the Creator of the Universe. A wonderful time is coming for us as the body of Messiah, the children of God. We will forever be singing His praises. We will do this in heaven around God's Throne.

Are Signs, Wonders, & Miracles for Today? Or for The Tribulation?

2 Thessalonians 2:9-12

9 Even him, whose coming is after the working of Satan with all power and signs and lying wonders,

10 And with all deceivableness of unrighteousness in them that perish; because they received not the love of the truth, that they might be saved.

11 And for this cause God shall send them strong delusion, that they should believe a lie:

12 That they all might be damned who believed not the truth but had pleasure in unrighteousness.

The world today looks for miracles, signs from the heavens, modern wonders, whether in the realm of religion or the secular, the world today is infatuated with modern day signs and miracles.

Today people claim they have seen apparitions of at Fatima, or statues of Jesus or Mary weeping blood. Many today believe we are being visited by other worldly beings because of unexplained lights in the heavens.

Even in some church circles today there are reports of Angel dust falling from the ceiling, people levitating, barking like dogs, which I believe is more subterfuge than truth. People want modern signs. God is a miracle working God, He still works miracles today. I am a miracle when He saved me and transformed my life. Israel is a modern miracle with its rebirth May 14, 1948, the Jews are a miracle of God.

However, Satan can also work miracles, false miracles, counterfeit miracles. Satan's greatest weapon is religion, and he knows how to use it very well! He is in the business of deception.

Therefore, Paul the Apostle warned the church at Thessaloniki when he said, "Let no man deceive you by any means" (2 Thess 2:3). The worst deception is self-deception. Satan is a master deceiver.

Even those within Christendom today claim they are receiving special revelation from God. That God is speaking audibly to them in a loud voice they hear with the naked ear. They prey on their emotions for financial gain.

The only revelation we have today is God's Word the Bible. We do not need any other so called modern-day revelation. When one claims modern-day revelation, they are false teachers.

Some in the church today claim Satan has no power to produce modern day miracles. This is not biblical. Satan is the prince and power of the air, (Eph 2:2), he is the god of this world, (2 Cor 4:4).

Paul said in 2 Corinthians 11:13-15 that Satan has the power to transform into whatever he wants, even an angel of light. His demons can do the same thing today. Satan also has his minions behind the pulpits of America and the world in the present.

13 For such [are] false apostles, deceitful workers, transforming themselves into the apostles of Christ.

14 And no marvel; for Satan himself is transformed into an angel of light.

15 Therefore [it is] no great thing if his ministers also be transformed as the ministers of righteousness; whose end shall be according to their works.

We have on Christian TV today false apostles and deceitful workers. Preying on the emotions of others for financial gain. Living high on the hog off the money of gullible people who give to them.

Satan has his ministers today teaching a false gospel in many churches. They pass themselves off as "ministers of righteousness". When, they are in fact disciples of the devil deceiving the masses. Are the signs, wonders, and miracles for today? Or, are they for the upcoming tribulation period? Many today would say, oh yes! But, there are no signs that precede the Rapture, no prophecies that must be fulfilled.

1. I am convinced Satan can perform lying miracles. He did it with Moses when Pharaoh's men turned their staffs into a serpent, (Exodus 7:11-12). It was a Satanic counterfeit miracle to deceive many. These signs, wonders, and miracles are not for today, but, for the 70th week of Daniel's prophecy, the future 7-year period of tribulation to come. Satan will perform one of his greatest counterfeit miracles.   After the Rapture, when the church is taken out of the world, Paul the Apostle tells us that the wicked one will be revealed, (2 Thess 2:8). When he is unveiled to the world Satan will energize him to be the Antichrist. Paul says in 2 Thessalonians 2:9 "even him (the Beast) whose coming is after the working of Satan with all power (authority), signs, and lying wonders. This man will deceive the world during the tribulation with satanic miracles.

In verse 10, it tells us the satanic trio of the tribulation, the Dragon, (Rev 12:3), the Beast, (Rev 13:1), and the False Prophet, (Rev 13:11), will deceive the globe by the means of these false miracles. The masses fall for these counterfeit miracles and swallow the lie of Satan and reject the truth of God's Word. Because of this, many perish in their sin and die without knowing the Lord as Savior.

In verse 11, God sends a strong delusion upon these individuals to believe Satan's lie. Why? These people had an opportunity to get saved in the church age and rejected that chance. They were not interested. They were left behind at the Rapture to swallow Satan's lie and die and go to hell for the rest of eternity.

Verse 12 says they believed not the truth but had pleasure in unrighteousness. Today, people have pleasure in unrighteousness. They love their sin. They love their immorality and will not exchange that for anything. When you speak against such sin the world looks at you like you're the walking plague.

We see in Revelation 13:13, Satan's end time miracle in the tribulation period. The Bible says the False Prophet, the second beast will do great wonders by calling down fire from heaven in the sight of men.

When he does this, verse 14 tells us he deceives the world by the means of these *miracles*. Yes, the Bible uses the word *miracle*. It is a satanic miracle to fool the earth-dwellers of the tribulation period.

In verse 15, the Antichrist makes an image of the Beast, a facsimile of himself. He speaks to that image and it comes to life speaking blasphemies against God. He demands the world worship this image.

We see in Revelation 16:13-14 John the Apostle said he saw three unclean spirits like frogs come out of the mouth of the Dragon, the Beast, and the False Prophet. The unholy trinity of the tribulation.

What is the purpose of these three unclean spirits coming out of the mouths of the terrible trio of the tribulation? (I love alliteration), according to verse 14, they are spirits of devils working miracles to deceive the kings of the earth.

Are signs, wonders, and miracles for today? No. They are for the tribulation period. You will have many signs in the tribulation period. Jesus speaks of false Christ's (Matt 24:5; 11; 24), who will deceive the very elect.

God is still using the gifts of the Spirit today among His true church to win precious souls to the Lord, to edify the body of

Messiah, to build up the Saints during the church age as we wait for Jesus return.

But, there are no sign, wonders, and miracles now, they will be however, in the tribulation period. Remember, no signs precede the Rapture, no prophecies must be fulfilled. We see last indicators that the end times are soon to come.

What is the Gap of Time Between The 69th And 70th Week of Daniel's Prophecy?

Daniel 9:24

"Seventy weeks are determined upon thy people and upon thy holy city, to finish the transgression, and to make an end of sins, and to make reconciliation for iniquity, and to bring in everlasting righteousness, and to seal up the vision and prophecy, and to anoint the most Holy.

The 70 Weeks of Daniel's Prophecy is considered one of the greatest mathematical prophecies in the entire word of God. It gives a precise timeline for the coming of Israel's Messiah and the Messiah's death.

If the Rabbis of the first century A.D. had been familiar with Daniel's timeline for the coming of the Messiah, if they would have studied Daniel 9, they would have had no issue identifying Jesus as the Messiah of Israel.

Daniel 9:24 tells us in the future, God will carry out the final week of Daniel's prophecy. This final week will come upon the Jews, as stated, *"thy people"*. We know it's the Jews because of the reference to, *"thy holy city"*, an obvious reference to Jerusalem.

In other words, a seven-year period of distress in the future will come upon Israel and the Jewish people. There is no reference to the church here since the church will not be in this time. In Daniel 9:24 we see three negatives and three positives in Daniel's prophecy. Three events that already transpired in the past, and three events that will happen in the future concerning Israel. The three negatives are: To finish the transgression, (Israel's rebellion), to make an end of sins, (Israel's sinful unregenerate state of unbelief), to make reconciliation for iniquity, (Messiah crucifixion). The three positives are: To bring in an everlasting righteousness, (Messiah's Kingdom), to seal up the vision and prophecy, (Daniel prophecies fulfilled and complete), and to anoint the Most Holy, (Messiah's reign as King of kings).

What we need to understand is that there is a gap of time in Daniel's prophecy between the 69th and the 70th week. That gap is found between Daniel 9: 26 and 27. Something paused the prophetic clock.

What paused the prophetic clock between verses 26 and 27 is the church. The church is between the gap of time. God placed the church between Daniel 9: 26 and 27. The church was not in the 69th week of Daniel, and the church will not be in the 70th week of Daniel in the future. The church is not found in the Old Testament, which in the Hebrew is הברית הישנה, "Havrit Heeshnah".

The church was a mystery. So, it makes sense that the church is found between verses 26 and 27. The church must fill that gap for an undetermined period before the Bride of Christ will be taken out of the world at the Rapture of the church. The church fills that gap of time in Daniel's prophecy.

For the 69 weeks of Daniel's prophecy, a 483-year period, or 178,880 days, during that time. God's prophetic calendar had a heartbeat. It was beating during the 69 weeks than it flatlined, it stopped beating.

The calendar flatlined for an undetermined period of time. Why did it flatline? God paused the calendar when He injected the church between the 69th and the 70th week of prophecy. We call this the church age.

The church age began at Pentecost in Acts 2 with the coming of the Holy Ghost upon 120 Jews at Jerusalem. We have been in the church age for nearly 2,000 years. The church age is what caused the flatline.

At the Rapture of the church, the next main event on God's calendar of events, when the church is removed the heartbeat will once again commence. When a person goes into cardiac arrest they use a Defibrillator to shock the heart to beat again.

At the Rapture, when the church is taken to heaven. God will cause the heartbeat of Daniel's prophecy to Defibrillate. The flatline will once again begin to pulse and show sign of life. That will be the 70th Week.

The mystery of the church is the gap of time. The mystery is something previously hidden, but now brought to life. This is the mystery of the church, (Eph 3:1-7; Col 1:24-29; Rom 16:25). The church is that gap.

The church as I said, was not in the 69th week, which commenced during the time of Nehemiah around 445 B.C to the cutting off of the Messiah in Daniel 9:26. This would be around 31-32 A.D. Jesus death ended the 69th week.

Nowhere is the church in that 69th week period. The 70th Week will happen sometime after the Rapture of the church. We call this the Pre-Tribulation Rapture. The church was not in the first period, nor in the future will it be in the second period.

The purpose of the tribulation is twofold and obvious. Number one, to come upon unbelieving Israel, which is why it is called a

"Time of Jacob's trouble", (Jer 30:7). Number two, to come upon the unbelieving nations of the world, (Matt 25).

In Matthew 25 we have the 10 Virgins, five wise and five unwise. This is Jewish people, the wise, saved Jews, the lost, unsaved Jews. Then, we have the sheep and goats, the sheep, saved Gentiles, the lost, unsaved Gentiles.

So, we have a parenthetical gap between the 69th and the 70th week of Daniel's prophecy. The gap is the present church age. Again, the prophetic heartbeat of the calendar flatlined with the insertion of the church between the 69th and 70th Week.

The Old Testament prophets had no idea, no revelation concerning the mystery of the church. It reminds us of the mountain peaks of prophecy in the Old Testament, they saw mountain tops, but not the valleys. The various mountain peaks would have been Jesus birth, (Mic 5:2) His death, (Ps 22; Isa 53), His resurrection, (Ps 16:10), His second coming, (Zech 14:4). The prophets clearly saw these prophecies.

However, the Jewish prophets could not see the valleys. What were those valleys? The church, the church age, and, the Rapture of the church. They did not see those valleys because it was a mystery to them.

Paul in his Epistles referred to the church as a 'mystery". If the church was in the Old Testament as some today wrongfully contend, Paul would have never used the term "mystery" to describe the church.

God his information on regarding the church age until the Apostle Paul. The church age will cease before the 70th Week of Daniel's prophecy. The church age closes at the Rapture of the church. Once the church is taken out, the heartbeat will resume. The flatline will begin to pulse, the heart will beat again during the tribulation period. Right now, we are in the pause period. The church age, that is about to end. Come soon Lord Jesus!

Why Reform Theology Leads to Anti-Israel Views

Romans 11:1-3; 12; 15; 23-24

1 I say then, Hath God cast away his people? God forbid. For I also am an Israelite, of the seed of Abraham, of the tribe of Benjamin.

2 God hath not cast away his people which he foreknew. Wot ye not what the scripture saith of Elias? how he maketh intercession to God against Israel, saying,

3 Lord, they have killed thy prophets, and digged down thine altars; and I am left alone, and they seek my life.

12 Now if the fall of them be the riches of the world, and the diminishing of them the riches of the Gentiles; how much more their fulness?

15 For if the casting away of them be the reconciling of the world, what shall the receiving of them be, but life from the dead?

23 And they also, if they abide not still in unbelief, shall be graffed in: for God is able to graff them in again.

24 For if thou wert cut out of the olive tree which is wild by nature, and wert graffed contrary to nature into a good olive tree: how much more shall these, which be the natural branches, be graffed into their own olive tree?

Romans 11 is a warning to Gentile believers concerning God's plan for Israel and the Jewish people. The chapter is designed to show that God has not abrogated His promises to the Jews.

During this dispensation God has temporarily laid Israel aside as He is dealing with the church during the church age to Evangelize the world in spreading the gospel.

Once the church is removed at the Rapture, God will than turn to Israel and deal with the Jewish people during the 70th Week of Daniel's prophecy, the "Time of Jacob's Trouble", Jeremiah 30:7,

"Alas! for that day is great, so that none is like it: it is even the time of Jacob's trouble; but he shall be saved out of it."

God will deal with Israel during the tribulation period, the 7-years of distress to bring them from unbelief, their current state, to belief in Jesus as Savior and Messiah.

When this happens, Israel will once again be restored as the head of nations and experience the blessings of God. All her original land grant will be restored.

The church does not supersede Israel. Paul the Apostle never uses that language in Romans 11. The church does not take over the promises God made to the Jews. The church and Israel are two distinct works of God.

Reform Theology is a system of interpreting the Bible allegorically, especially when dealing with Israel and Eschatology. They spiritualize the literal promises God made with the Jews and transfer them to the church.

In Romans 11 Paul is dealing with national and not individual destiny. He is dealing with national Israel here; the context is so clear. It is the national election of Israel.

Paul is not dealing with individual destiny or individual salvation, as reform theologians try to teach. You have the national election of Israel and the ecclesiastical election of the church.

Calvinist try to cease on this and apply this passage to individual salvation. This is a wrong Hermeneutical principle. Bible allegorizing is very dangerous. It leads to the reader determining what he thinks the Scriptures should say.

Paul never deals with individuals here, he is dealing with national Israel. And Paul shows that God has nor terminated His future program for national Israel. Despite their unbelief, God has not cast them away. Paul shows that despite Israel's unbelief they will be restored to future national blessings from God.

Reform theology contradicts this and says God is finished with Israel, the church has replaced her. We call this, "Replacement Theology", or Supersessionism.

Reform theology is also known as "Covenant Theology", and sees God washing His hands of the Jews. They see no future restoration for Israel, they see all of God's promises for the Jews as null and void.

Romans 11 puts this to rest and shows that God is not done with Israel. The Bible anticipates the present spiritual condition of Israel as it is today, as it's been for the past 2,000 years, unbelief.

The Jews are back in the land as foretold by the Jewish prophets but back in unbelief, (Rom 11:25). This unbelief will reach its height at the halfway point of the tribulation when they see they were wrong.

The Jews will flee for their lives when the Antichrist breaks the conformation peace treaty in Daniel 9:27. They will flee to the mountains, Petra, where God will supernaturally protect them for the last half of Daniel's 70th Week.

Why is Reform Theology becoming so prevalent in the church today? Why are many Christians spiritualizing the literal promises of God for the Jews and transferring them to the church?

It is due to the problem of Anti-Semitism. Yes, Anti-Semitism is a major problem in the church today. I have seen it up close and personal. Because of Reform theology, Christians are seeing Israel in a negative light.

When you fail to take the Scriptures for their Grammatical, contextual, historical, and very important, literal interpretation, we will fall for every wind of doctrine. Reform theology fails to interpret the plain sense interpretation of Scripture.

The one who allegorize Scripture is in control and brings his own thoughts and ideas to the table. What he thinks the Bible should say. That's why its "reform" theology. They reform the Bible to make it fit their doctrine.

The Times of Israel reported on January 11, 2018, "Support for Israel Among Young Evangelicals Dips". According to the report the reason for this drop is the failure to take the Scriptures literally.

Because of this failure to literally interpret the Bible, many young Christians have become ambivalent to Israel, to God's literal promises to the Jews. Reform theology has muddied the waters in terms of God's future program for the Jews.

Many millennials within the church have an anti-view of Israel. You have so called church leaders like Tony Campolo who are Pro-Palestinian and condemn the teaching of Bible prophecy and pro-Israel support.

Paul is unambiguous in saying that God is not finished with Israel, (11:1-2). Paul says in verse 11 that Israel has stumbled, but not to the point that they are completely out of God's program, verse 12 says they will be restored.

11 I say then, Have they stumbled that they should fall? God forbid: but [rather] through their fall salvation [is come] unto the Gentiles, for to provoke them to jealousy.

12 Now if the fall of them [be] the riches of the world, and the diminishing of them the riches of the Gentiles; how much more their fulness? (future restoration).

Paul warns the Gentiles not to boast concerning Israel's temporary fall, yet Gentiles in the church today are doing exactly that! Paul shows Israel's blindness and rejection of Jesus is temporary.

Clearly, Romans 11 sees a future national restoration of Israel. Ezekiel 36 sees this as well. We see salvation came to the Gentiles because of Israel's fall in verse 11, but we also see a restoration in Romans 11:15.

"For if the casting away of them be the reconciling of the world, what shall the receiving of them be, but life from the dead?" (future restoration).

The broken branches are the Jews, the wild olive trees the Gentiles, the root is Israel. The wild olive tree reaps the benefits of the natural branches of the root. Paul never says the Olive tree supersedes the natural Branches, (Jews).

The branches were broken off, (Israel set aside), the olive tree (Gentiles) is enjoying the fatness of the

root. Paul does not see any usurping here by either the Branches or the wild olive tree. Paul sees national restoration of Israel in Romans11:23,

"And they also, if they abide not still in unbelief, shall be graffed in: for God is able to graff them in again.

This happens at Jesus second coming to earth at the end of Daniel's 70th Week, (Zech 12:10; Rom 11:26; Matt 24:30; Rev 1:7). Israel will come to the end of themselves and call upon the Name of Jesus, (Joel 2:32).

Therefore, we should take the Scriptures literally, allow the Bible to interpret the Bible. We call this inductive Bible study. When we allegorize Scripture, we make it become subjective, we must be objective when it comes to the study of God's Word.

God has a plan for Israel, He has a plan for the church. Neither supersedes the other. God will deal with Israel in the future once the church has been taken out at the Rapture. God will deal with the Jews in the 70th week.

Israel is only temporarily set aside. Her blindness and rejection temporal only. God will fulfill his promises to her. Bible prophecy will be fulfilled. The Rapture is the next main event!

The First & Second Resurrection

Revelation 20:5-6

5 But the rest of the dead lived not again until the thousand years were finished. This [is] the first resurrection.

6 Blessed and holy [is] he that hath part in the first resurrection: on such the second death hath no power, but they shall be priests of God and of Christ and shall reign with him a thousand years.

The Bible clearly speaks of a first and second resurrection in the future. A first resurrection that leads to life and a second resurrection that leads to damnation. We see this mentioned in both Testaments.

Many get confused over this topic and others see a general resurrection with God judging Christians and unbelievers at the same time. The Bible does not teach a general judgment or resurrection.

John the Apostle sees the dead being raised after the one thousand years are complete. John calls this the first resurrection. I struggled with this passage for years and tried to figure out who the dead are here.

The rest of the dead would refer to the unsaved dead, the unbelievers who died in their sin and went to the temporary holding place called hell. Hell holds them for the final judgment after the 1000 years are complete.

My issue with that passage was, how can the unsaved dead take part in the first resurrection? If the first resurrection is a resurrection to life, how can unbelievers take part in that? I looked at commentaries and other explanations with no answer.

We know the book of Revelation must be read chronologically. We must look at it in chronological order to understand this majestic apocalyptic filled book. It is a book of apocalyptic literature.

The Bible speaks of various resurrections in Scripture concerning certain groups. You have the resurrection of Jesus from the dead, you have the resurrection of the church, you have the resurrection of the Two Witnesses.

You have the resurrection of Old Testament Saints, you have the Resurrection of Tribulation martyrs, and, you have the resurrection of unbelievers to stand before Jesus at the Great White Throne Judgment.

We know that Jesus is the first fruits of the resurrection, (1 Cor 15:20). He conquered death by rising from the dead. He overcame death, something no one else has ever done. He physically and bodily rose from the dead.

Jesus became the First Fruits of them that slept. Them who have fallen asleep. Sleep is a metaphor for death in the Bible. The First Fruits were the third Feast in Leviticus 23, and it always anticipated a grain harvest in Israel.

Jesus was the first to rise, He rose by the power of the Holy Spirit, yet, Jesus said in John 10:17-18 "*I lay down my life, that I might take it again, I have power to lay it down I have power to take it again*".

There is an order we must follow according to 1 Corinthians 15:23, "*But every man in his own order*". Jesus resurrection is the first, and in the future, there will be other resurrections to follow in order.

The second resurrection to follow will be the resurrection of the Saints, we call this the Rapture of the church. Again, Paul the Apostle said in verse 23, "*afterward they that are Christ's at His coming*".

When Jesus comes for His church at the Rapture, believers will also experience resurrection. The two Rapture passages are 1

Corinthians 15:51-52 and 1 Thessalonians 4:13-18. This the first half of the first resurrection.

The second half of the first resurrection will involve the raising of Old Testament Saints and Tribulation Saints. They will be raised at the end of the tribulation prior to the inauguration of the Kingdom.

The passages for the raising of Old Testament Saints are Isaiah 26:19 and Daniel 12:2. These Old Testament Saints trusted in the Lord prior to the death, burial, and resurrection of Jesus from the dead.

We see the resurrection of tribulation Saints from the dead, those who lost their lives during Daniel's 70th Week of prophecy. They will be raised as well to enter the Kingdom along with Old Testament Saints, (Luke 19:12-27; Rev 20:4).

Luke 19:12-27 record the raising of tribulation Saints. The raising of both these groups will complete the first resurrection. Remember, the first half of the first resurrection involves Jesus and the church, the last half of the first resurrection involves the raising of Old Testament and Tribulation Saints.

This brings us back to Revelation 20:5-6, "But the rest of the dead lived not again until the thousand years were finished. This is the first resurrection". As I said, I struggled with this for years and could not understand this.

A reading of this should be approached chronologically. The first half of verse 5 is a parenthesis and comes chronologically after Revelation 20:11. This is the Great White Throne Judgment of the unbelievers.

The last half of verse five chronologically backs up and is equivalent to Revelation 20:4. Verse 4 records the resurrection of those tribulation martyrs who will live and reign with Christ 1000 years.

At the end of the 1000-year reign of Jesus in the Davidic Theocratic Kingdom, the unbelievers will be summoned from hell that now holds them, and they will stand before Jesus at the Great White Throne.

The resurrection of the unsaved dead is the Second Resurrection. It is a resurrection to damnation. The second resurrection is known as the Second Death. There is a physical death and a second death.

The books, (plural) contain the deeds of the unsaved from the womb to the tomb. These books testify against them, that they are guilty as charged. The Book (singular) is the Book of Life that contain the names of the redeemed.

Revelation 20:14 tells us that death and hell were cast into the Lake of Fire, this is the second death. These unbelievers were cast into the Lake of fire. They will forever experience the second death. I heard one preacher say, "If your born twice, you'll die once, if your born once, you'll die twice". The second death in the Lake of fire. It is an eternal death the unsaved will experience for all eternity.

My question for you today is, what resurrection will you experience? A resurrection that leads to eternal life? Or, a resurrection that leads to eternal damnation? Which is it for you? The first or second resurrection?

Trust in the Lord Jesus as your personal Savior and be ready to participate in that first resurrection. Jesus was the First Fruits of the resurrection. Next up in order, the church at the Rapture. The dead and Christ and living Saints will be caught up!

37

Notes

Does the Rare Moon Signal the End of Islam's Dominance of The Temple Mount?

Joel 3:15

15 The sun and the moon shall be darkened, and the stars shall withdraw their shining.

The Bible sees a time when the heavens will go into a violent apocalyptic convulsion during the Day of the Lord to come upon humanity. It will be signs in the sun, the moon, and the stars.

We see in Joel, Luke, and the book of Revelation, where the heavens will erupt into a chaotic scene that will terrify the inhabitants of the earth. Nothing like this has ever been seen before and it will shake humanity to its core.

There have been all types of rare occurrences in the heavens with blood moons and blue moons and super moons during the church age. Many have tried to tie these rare occurrences as present apocalyptic judgements.

Many "Prophecy" teachers have cashed in with writing books on these rare moons, whether blood moons or Super moons, and say they are signs for Israel, when these moons were not even seen in Israel.

John Hagee had the church reeling with his book, "Four Blood Moons" in which he said they are major apocalyptic signs for Israel with the fourth moon bringing something catastrophic. Nothing happened.

This fourth moon was not even seen in the holy land. Again, none of these rare moons over the years were seen in Israel, yet, they claim they were major signs for Israel. Mark Biltz, a Hebrew Roots Movement leader with strange doctrines claimed he originated the Blood Moons theory and threatened to sue Hagee.

The bottom line is this, nothing happened of an apocalyptic nature, and Hagee laughed all the way to the bank, raking in hundreds of thousands of dollars, leaving the poor deluded

Christian disappointed. When will we stop drinking the Eschatological Kool Aid?

Even with the rare Super blue moon in January of 2018, many so called Prophecy teachers and people on Facebook were trying to tie this Super Moon with Joel's Prophecy in Joel chapters 2 and 3.

The problem with these so-called prophecy teachers is that they are trying to take Joel's prophecy of the moon being turned into blood and put that prophecy as a fulfillment in the present church age. This is a wrong biblical Hermeneutic. That prophecy in Joel is still future, it is not taking place in the present as many are trying to say with these rare moon occurrences. We must keep Joel's prophecy as Eschatological, an event that is still future.

The Breaking Israel News Website reported the rare Super Blue Moon converged with the Jewish holiday of Tu B'Shvat, the planting of trees in Israel. According to several ancient Jewish sources, this rare moon in conjunction with Tu B'Shvat spells the end of Ishmael's reign on the Temple Mount.

According to Rabbi Berger, the Chief Rabbi at the traditional tomb of king David on Mt. Zion. He said a 124-year-old Jewish source foretold a rare moon that will coincide with Tu B' Shvat will usher in intensified earthquakes worldwide.

This dire prediction was also foretold in the Talmud that a lunar eclipse is a bad omen for Jews, but Israel will not be affected since the eclipse will not be visible in Israel. But will affect Arab countries.

According to these Rabbis this lunar eclipse signals the beginning of a harsh period for the Bnei Ishmael, (Sons of Ishmael), which is necessary for the coming of the Meshiach, or Messiah.

Rabbi Berger explained that the connection between the fall of the Arabs and the arrival of the Messiah was by Rabbi Jacob Ben Asher, a 13th century A.D. biblical commentator in his explanation of Genesis 25:18;

"And they dwelt from Havilah unto Shur, that is before Egypt, as thou goest toward Assyria: and he died in the presence of all his brethren."

The Rabbi explained, because Ishmael died, the Bible verse is adjacent to the verse describing the life of Isaac, to teach that when Ishmael falls, it will be in the end of days, and the son of David, the Messiah, who descends from Isaac, will flourish. The Rabbi explained, just as the Exodus to freedom required harsh judgment to fall on Egypt for oppressing the Jews and prevented us from serving God, the same is true today concerning the Arabs.

The Rabbi said, "For the Jews to return to the Temple, the Arabs who treated the Jews badly and prevented us from serving God must have a judgment brought upon them". According to Bible prophecy, that will happen.

Ezekiel 38 describes a Russian led Arab coalition of nations to attack Israel. Ezekiel 39:2 tells us a sixth part of this coalition will be destroyed. In other words, 5/6th of the Arabs are wiped out, five out of every six Muslims.

Ezekiel 35, Obadiah 15-19, and Malachi 1 tell us the Palestinians will be destroyed when they make their move against the Jewish people to kill the Jews and take their land. Psalm 83 records the Arab confederacy being wiped out when they attack Israel.

Prior to the coming of Jesus, the Messiah the heavens will convulse violently, Joel 2:30-31 describes signs in the heavens, blood, fire, pillars of smoke, the sun being darkened and the moon into blood,

30 And I will shew wonders in the heavens and in the earth, blood, and fire, and pillars of smoke.

31 The sun shall be turned into darkness, and the moon into blood, before the great and the terrible day of the LORD come.

Jesus in Luke 21:25-26 speaks of signs in the sun, moon, and stars, upon the earth distress of nations, men's heart's failing them for fear of those things coming on the earth with the powers of heaven being shaken,

25 And there shall be signs in the sun, and in the moon, and in the stars; and upon the earth distress of nations, with perplexity; the sea and the waves roaring;

26 Men's hearts failing them for fear, and for looking after those things which are coming on the earth: for the powers of heaven shall be shaken.

In Revelation 6:12, the moon turns to blood with the opening of the sixth seal. In Revelation 8:12, the third part of the sun and moon were smitten causing total darkness. The point to all this is that this is future. This is apocalyptic in nature that unfolds during Daniel's 70th Week of prophecy, not in the present with these rare moon occurrences. Stop trying to put these future events in the present because of Super Moons or total lunar Eclipses.

When Jesus returns at tribulation's end He will reign from the Temple Mount in Jerusalem on David's Throne with a Millennial Temple standing on the most sacred piece of Real Estate today.

We see last days indicators the end times are coming. But, there are no prophecies that must be fulfilled before the Rapture, no signs precede the Rapture. It is an event that is imminent.

The Arabs will lose control of the Temple Mount in the future when they come against Israel.

Dark Doctrines of Demons

Galatians 1:8-9

8 But though we, or an angel from heaven, preach any other gospel unto you than that which we have preached unto you, let him be accursed.

9 As we said before, so say I now again, If any [man] preach any other gospel unto you than that ye have received, let him be accursed.

Paul the Apostle warned the church at Galatia about "false gospels" being propagated by false religions, cults, the Judaizers that were oppressing the Galatians, even converting some them.

Paul warns about the preaching of another "gospel", whether it came from the Apostle himself, an angel, or anyone for that matter preaching another gospel that differs from the biblical gospel, that person is accursed.

If someone is preaching error that is foreign from Scripture they are to be accursed, that is eternally condemned. Their doctrine is accursed, and they are accursed as well as those they convert to follow them.

The other time we find this word "accursed" is in 1 Corinthians 16:22 where Paul tells us if any man love not our Lord Jesus let him be "Anathema", another word for accursed. All false doctrines are anathema, *"If any man love not the Lord Jesus Christ, let him be Anathema Maranatha."*

Paul reiterates again in Galatians 1:9, he wants his hearers to listen very carefully as to how important this is. Souls are at stake! People are following false teachers, they are everywhere, in the church, outside the church, social media.

The Apostle wants to show that the Message, not the messenger is of the utmost importance. When the messenger wants to make it all about him, a red flag should go off in your head. When they say salvation comes from their church or organization only, run for the hills!

The Galatian controversy, and there were many, was not over teachers or personalities, but over truth and error. The Galatians were dealing with error in their midst. False teachers were coming in and deceiving the flock.

Some 2,000 years later, the problem continues to persist, even many Christians today are fallen into error by following certain personalities on television and failing to read the Bible, they are failing to get their doctrine from God's Word.

If we fail to get our doctrine from Scripture and take some TV personality's word for it, we will get into doctrinal trouble. When he makes it all about him, his message all about him, something is wrong here. Religious leaders of cults have done for this from time immemorial. They must make it all about them and not about the Lord Jesus. They must be above the Lord and must have the preeminence over the people.

The case in point was a man in the church Bible describes as Diotrephes. This man wanted it to be all about him. He wanted people to focus on him and not on the Lord Jesus. This man was dangerous. When John the Apostle exposed him, he had John and other believers thrown out of the church. We See in 3 John 9, *"I wrote unto the church: but Diotrephes, who loveth to have the preeminence among them, receiveth us not."*

I had to deal with a guy on Facebook who said that salvation comes through his church only. When I challenged him on this through Scripture, that Jesus is the only way to heaven, and that Salvation is through Him alone, the man laughed. Paul said that in the last days they would have a "form of godliness, but denying the power thereof, from such turn away" (2 Tim 3:5). They have a deceptive form of godliness, they look real but are counterfeit Christians, *"Having a form of godliness, but denying the power thereof: from such turn away."*

In Acts 20:29 Paul said that after he moves out the wolves will move in. Veteran preachers have been dying off and young preachers coming out of liberal Bible schools taken over churches and mislead the flock, *"For I know this, that after my departing shall grievous wolves enter in among you, not sparing the flock."*

Jesus said the same thing about false teachers, using the analogy of wolves coming in sheep's clothing, passing themselves off as legitimate preachers of the gospel. Jesus expressed this in Matthew 7:15-16;

15 Beware of false prophets, which come to you in sheep's clothing, but inwardly they are ravening wolves.

16 Ye shall know them by their fruits. Do men gather grapes of thorns, or figs of thistles?

Jesus said in Matthew 7:15 that we are to beware of false prophets that come in sheep's clothing. They come in the form of Jehovah's Witnesses, the Mormons, Roman Catholicism, or any cult that depart from Scripture. I would even be criticized by some Christians and church leaders for that matter for naming Catholicism. I am here to speak truth and not to win a popularity contest. The Message is about Jesus, not me the messenger.

The Times of Israel reported about the Mormon cult performing proxy baptisms at the graves of Jewish holocaust victims to give the deceased in the afterlife a chance to accept or reject salvation that comes through Mormonism.

Many Jews have been outraged and family members sickened to their stomach and rightfully so. It is nothing but an insult to the victims of mass genocide by the Nazi regime. This proxy baptism of the dead is from the pit of hell.

These deceived followers of Joseph Smith are posthumously baptizing Jewish holocaust victims. They have been practicing this false doctrine for years. The proxy baptism is supposed to convert the dead to Mormonism.

According to the so-called church of Jesus Christ of Latter Day Saints, the proxy baptisms give the deceased a choice to accept or reject the offer of baptism or salvation that comes only from this cult.

Mormonism is the only religious cult that baptizes the dead. Since the 1990's, the Mormon cult has performed a few hundred thousand proxy baptisms on Jewish Holocaust victims which is grossly insensitive.

In 1995, the LDS barred the baptisms of Jewish holocaust victims as well as celebrities. The LDS performed a proxy baptism on Anne Frank. The LDS even perform this unbiblical practice on living non-Mormons to get them out of "spirit prison." The reason this cult does this is because they say, "God wants all His children home again, in families and in glory."

What God are they talking about? Mormonism is a Polytheistic cult, the belief in many gods.

There is a saying in Mormonism, "as man is God once was, as God is man will someday be". They believe Jesus and the devil were brothers. The Bible has been corrupted over the centuries and replaced by the book of Mormon.

Mormons believe they will become gods one day. This is the lie the serpent told Adam and Eve in the garden, *"Ye shall be as gods knowing good and evil"* (Gen 3:5). The Mormons have swallowed this lie from Satan.

Paul the Apostle warned about baptizing the dead. Paul says what is the purpose of baptizing dead people if the dead rise not? Paul is arguing the for the future resurrection, but the

Mormons take this out of context. Paul is simply saying, "baptized in place of" younger converts taking the place of older ones who passed on in service in the church.

In the last days in which we live the cults will intensify their activity that will pave the way for the end times to commence sometime after the Rapture. The end time false church of Revelation 17 will be in cahoots with the Antichrist.

With these false cults and their unbiblical doctrines and practices being practiced worldwide, Bible prophecy is on course to being fulfilled and the Rapture of the church about to happen very soon!

Notes

The Metamorphosis Experience
Matthew 17: 1-4

1 And after six days Jesus taketh Peter, James, and John his brother, and bringeth them up into an high mountain apart,

2 And was transfigured before them: and his face did shine as the sun, and his raiment was white as the light.

3 And, behold, there appeared unto them Moses and Elias talking with him.

4 Then answered Peter, and said unto Jesus, Lord, it is good for us to be here: if thou wilt, let us make here three tabernacles; one for thee, and one for Moses, and one for Elias.

Matthew 17 records the transformation of Jesus while He and His Disciples were on a very high mountain. There are two mountains in Israel that are said to be the sight of this event, Mount Tabor and Mount Hermon.

Mt. Tabor is in the lower Galilee and is 1,886 feet high. Mount Hermon is in the Golan Heights and is 9,232 feet high. The mountain is known as the eyes of Israel. The IDF has a military station located there.

It seems more likely that Mount Hermon is the location for the event that happened in Matthew 17. Matthew says Jesus took the Disciples, Peter, James, and John to a high mountain, Mt. Hermon would be that mountain.

Peter, James, and John would be known as the inner circle of leadership among the twelve Disciples. It was the same three who were with Jesus in the Garden of Gethsemane in Matthew 26:37.

We see three parallel passages for this event, Matthew 17, Mark 9, and Luke 9. We see in Matthew 17:1 where it says,

"And after six days". Six days earlier Jesus and the Disciples are at Caesarea Philippi in Matthew 16.

Caesarea Philippi lies at the foot of Mount Hermon in the Golan Heights. So, we know once again that Mount Hermon is the location of the Transfiguration. It was at Caesarea Philippi that Peter confesses Jesus to be the Messiah.

Six days later they are on Mount Hermon and Jesus is transfigured before them. The verb is the Greek *Metamorphoo* which indicates a transformation of essential form proceeding from within. A change from the inside out.

When we come to faith in Jesus there is a spiritual *metamorphoo*, a metamorphosis that happens within us when Jesus transforms us from old to new, (2 Cor 5:17). We are also changed from the inside out.

To be transfigured means to be altered in form. In Luke 9:27 Jesus told the Disciples they would not taste of death until they see the Kingdom of God. They did! At the Transfiguration on Mt. Hermon.

Matthew 17: 2 says *"His face did shine as the sun, and His raiment was white as light"*. Mark 9:3 tells us, *"And His raiment became shining, exceeding white as snow;"*. Luke 9:29 says *"the fashion of His countenance was altered, and His raiment was white and glistering"*.

Jesus while on earth veiled His glory. He veiled His Deity. The only time Jesus un-veiled His Deity is at the Transfiguration. Paul the Apostle refers to this in Philippians 2:7 where Jesus took upon Him the form of a servant and was made in the likeness of men,

"But made himself of no reputation, and took upon him the form of a servant, and was made in the likeness of men:"

The Greek word here is *Kenosis* and means "emptying" and is related to the verb Translated. When Paul said Jesus made Himself of no reputation, he literally meant, "emptied Himself". He did this by veiling His glory.

On Mt. Hermon the Disciples saw a preview of the Kingdom before they died. They saw the Lord in His Kingdom Glory. The promise of the Davidic Theocratic Kingdom to come as foretold by the Jewish prophets.

It will be a Kingdom ruled by the Messiah, the Son of the living God as confessed by Peter six days earlier at Caesarea Philippi. He will reign from David's Throne in Jerusalem for 1000 years, (Rev 20:2-7).

Jesus walked the holy land, the land of Israel 2,000 years ago as the Man-God, the Son of Man, as He is called some 79 times in the New Testament. Jesus had two natures, He was fully man and fully God.

We call this the "Hypostatic Union". Jesus had two natures, He was man without the taint of original sin and He was God Almighty, Creator of heaven and earth. He was the perfect sinless Son of Man. The Lamb of God, (John 1:29; 36).

We see another event, this time in heaven involving John the Apostle in the book of Revelation concerning the Glory of Jesus the Messiah. John sees Jesus in heaven in His Glorified State.

We see in Revelation 1:13-16 the only snapshot of Jesus in the Bible. The only biblical description we have of Jesus. John describes His head and hairs as white as wool, just like snow, His eyes being a flame of fire,

13 And in the midst of the seven candlesticks [one] like unto the Son of man, clothed with a garment down to the foot, and girt about the paps with a golden girdle.

14 His head and [his] hairs [were] white like wool, as white as snow; and his eyes [were] as a flame of fire;

15 And his feet like unto fine brass, as if they burned in a furnace; and his voice as the sound of many waters.

16 And he had in his right hand seven stars: and out of his mouth went a sharp twoedged sword: and his countenance [was] as the sun shineth in his strength.

John describes His feet as fine brass as if they burned in a furnace and His voice as the sound of many waters. If you have ever been to Niagara Falls the water falls are deafening. You can barely hear yourself.

John in verse 16 describes the Lord's countenance as the sun shining in its strength. John had the privilege to see this twice, on Mt. Hermon in the Golan Heights in Israel and in heaven as he saw this event.

During His earthly ministry John saw the Lord Jesus in His Veiled Glory with an exception at the Transfiguration. Then, John sees Jesus in heaven with His Glory Un-Veiled in Majesty and power.

One day the church will be changed from mortal to immortality at the Rapture of the church. Paul said in 1 Corinthians 15:51-52 that we shall all be changed, transfigured, *Metamorphoo*, at the translation of the church, the Rapture,

51 Behold, I shew you a mystery; We shall not all sleep, but we shall all be changed,

52 In a moment, in the twinkling of an eye, at the last trump: for the trumpet shall sound, and the dead shall be raised incorruptible, and we shall be changed.

Colossians 1:13 tells us we as the church have been delivered from the power of darkness and translated us into the Kingdom of His Dear Son. We have been transferred from one state to another,

"Who hath delivered us from the power of darkness, and hath translated us into the kingdom of his dear Son:"

The writer in Hebrews 11:5 said by faith Enoch was translated that he should not see death. God had translated him. Before his translation he had this testimony, that he pleased God. In that verse we see <u>translated</u> mentioned twice, and <u>translation</u> mentioned once. This goes back to Genesis 5:24,

Genesis 5:24

"And Enoch walked with God: and he was not; for God took him."

Hebrews 11:5

"By faith Enoch was translated that he should not see death; and was not found, because God had translated him: for before his translation he had this testimony, that he pleased God."

One day we will be translated, we will be metamorphic in transition from sinful to sinless, from mortal to immortal, from corruptible to incorruptible, with a glorified body at the Rapture of the church.

The Rapture could happen at any moment! Not only has Jesus changed us now, but, He will change us in the future, and we will be translated to heaven at the Blessed Hope, the coming of Jesus for His Bride.

Whatever Happened to The Doctrine of The Rapture?

Revelation 1:3

"Blessed is he that readeth, and they that hear the words of this prophecy, and keep those things which are written therein: for the time is at hand."

What happened to the doctrine of the Rapture? Why aren't churches teaching this doctrine of the Blessed Hope? Why are churches by and large ignoring an important truth that permeates one third of Scripture?

The arguments today by some Christians are, the word Rapture does not appear in the Bible, well, the word trinity, demons, and Bible, don't appear in the Bible either, but we believe in these doctrines.

All because a word does not appear in the Bible does not mean the doctrine is not there. We are slowly killing the doctrine of the Rapture and Pastors are robbing their people of the doctrine of the Blessed Hope by failing to preach it.

The Doctrine of the Blessed Hope is what motivates us as believers to live a life of holy conduct in a world of sinfulness and rebellion against God. To Evangelize and win people to the Lord before it's too late.

Titus 2:13 tells us to look for the blessed hope, and the glorious appearing of our great God and Savior Jesus Christ. In that verse we have the Rapture and the second coming, to distinct events in Scripture,

"Looking for that blessed hope, and the glorious appearing of the great God and our Saviour Jesus Christ;"

Many Christians today get confused and don't differentiate between the Rapture and the second coming. At the Rapture, Jesus comes for His church, at the second coming, He returns with His church.

The doctrine of the Rapture in some cases is disliked among Evangelical circles. I have heard the Rapture doctrine ridiculed and Rapture passages spiritualized to try to strip the text of its true meaning.

I spoke at a Messianic Jewish Congregation in Indiana where a friend mine said some Christians will not show up because they heard I was teaching on the Rapture. He was heartbroken, we still had a service.

We must not forget that the Rapture is a major doctrine in the Word of God, and it is incumbent upon us to teach and preach that doctrine, but we must understand that event to do so.

The word Rapture does not appear in the Bible. It comes from the Latin word *Raptura* which means to seize or snatch away. The Greek word *Harpazo* does appear in Scripture and has the same connotation as *Raptura*. Harpazo means to harpoon. You harpoon a something and bring it in. One Day the church will be harpooned and taken to heaven.

The doctrine is found in 1 Thessalonians 4:17, *"Then we which are alive and remain shall be <u>caught up</u> together with them in the clouds, to meet the Lord in the air: and so shall we ever be with the Lord."*

Notice the word *"caught up"*. That is *Harpazo* in the Greek, to harpoon and reel in. It is Rapturo in Latin, to snatch away, it is the first person plural future indicative passive tense to be precise. It is clearly taught in the Bible.

There are two main passages in the New Testament for the Rapture, 1 Thessalonians 4:16-18 and 1 Corinthians 15:51-52. Jesus will descend from heaven with a shout, the voice of the Archangel, and the blowing of the Shofar, (Trumpet) to call all true believers home.

There are no signs that precede this event, no prophecies that must be fulfilled. The Rapture is imminent, simply meaning, something hanging over our heads ready to befall us, ready to overtake us.

We will be changed in a twinkling of an eye. Changed instantly from mortal to immortal, from perishable to imperishable, from corruptible to incorruptible, our sin nature is eradicated, and we will receive a glorified body at the Rapture.

Paul refers to this again to the church at Philippi in Philippians 3:20-21 as to believers receiving a glorified body at the Rapture of the church. Our vile sinful corrupt bodies will be changed when He comes,

20 For our conversation is in heaven; from whence also we look for the Saviour, the Lord Jesus Christ:

21 Who shall change our vile body, that it may be fashioned like unto his glorious body, according to the working whereby he is able even to subdue all things unto himself.

John the Baptist in John 3: 28-30 refers to Jesus as the Bride and the church as the Bridegroom. Even though the phrase "Bride of Christ" does not appear in Scripture, the idea is strongly implied in the Bible that church is the Bride of Messiah.

Jesus will return for His Bride, He is the head of the body, the church, (Eph 5:23). He will take His church out of this world before the Eschatological events unfold on planet earth during the events of Daniel's 70th Week of Prophecy.

The church will be delivered at the Rapture before the tribulation period. There is no reason whatsoever for the church to be in the 70th week of prophecy. The church was not in the 69th week and will not be in the 70th week.

The Bible strongly implies the church is taken out before the 70th week, (Rom 5:9; 1 Thess 1:10; 5:9; Rev 3:10). The tribulation period is a time of Jacob's Trouble, (Jer 30:7), not the "church's trouble.

Some who hold to other Rapture positions claim the church must go through the tribulation period to be purified, that is creating a Protestant Purgatory, that's foolish! The church is purified by the blood of the Lamb, (1 John 1:7; 1 Peter 1:18-19; Hebrews 9:14).

Another fallacy argument is why should God only deliver Christians from the tribulation since we are still sinful? Because we accepted His payment of forgiveness and trusted him as Savior, those left behind did not.

Today we are in the church age, we are in the age of grace. We have had 2,000 years of church age history. During this age we fulfill the great commission of preaching the gospel to every creature.

Unfortunately, the great commission has become the great Omission. We are failing to share the gospel because of fear and intimidation. Christians by and large have no problem fighting on Facebook over doctrine while souls slip into hell. We are no longer yearning, but, yawning, concerning Jesus return.

The church age began at Pentecost and will end at the Rapture of the church. God is dealing with the church now as Israel is temporarily set aside; the job of the church is to evangelize the world with the good news of the gospel.

When the Rapture takes place and the church is taken out, God will deal with Israel during the 70th Week of Daniel's prophecy to bring them to faith in Yeshua as Messiah and Savior, as well as the unbelieving Gentile nations.

The Rapture is a biblical doctrine. It is the Blessed Hope of the Christian, and a doctrine you can believe in. Jesus promised He will come again, (John 14:1-3). Jesus is God and He cannot lie.

Why the Additional Days in Daniel's Prophecy?

Daniel 12:11-12

11 And from the time [that] the daily [sacrifice] shall be taken away, and the abomination that maketh desolate set up, [there shall be] a thousand two hundred and ninety days.

12 Blessed [is] he that waiteth, and cometh to the thousand three hundred and five and thirty days.

The closing passages of the book of Daniel has been one of the most controversial text among scholars and Bible prophecy teachers. Many are left scratching their heads and saying, what does it mean?

Daniel is showing us that there are additional days added to the original days of the 70th Week of Daniel's prophecy. Why the additional days to this prophecy have many wondering, Why the additional days?

The Jewish prophet Daniel was a captive of Babylon and the prophet of the Babylonian captivity. In 605 B.C Daniel was taking from Jerusalem along with his three Jewish friends, Hananiah, Mishael, and Azariah.

Daniel was probably very young when he was taken to Babylon 605 years before the birth of Jesus the Messiah. He was taken during Nebuchadnezzar's first wave of invasion against Jerusalem. Ezekiel was taken in 597 B.C during Babylon's second invasion. Daniel and Ezekiel were the Jewish prophets of the exile.

The third and final invasion came in 586 B.C. when the Babylonians destroyed Jerusalem and Solomon's Temple, and took the Jews back to Babylon for the 70 years of captivity. 1. Daniel and Ezekiel were known as the Jewish prophets of the captivity. Daniel was about 15 years old when he was taken in 605 B.C., and by the time we get to chapter 12 he is about 85 years old.

Daniel is one of those Apocalyptic books that uses Apocalyptic literature. Daniel uses symbols to convey an absolute truth. There is a literal interpretation behind these symbols and the Bible itself will interpret those symbols. Daniel gives us the timeline for the Gentiles and Ezekiel the timeline for the Jews.

The book of Daniel is also not in Chronological order. That means as you read the book you must jump from chapter to chapter to understand what Daniel is saying. So, don't read Daniel numerically, but, Chronologically. So, how do we read Daniel Chronologically? We read the Chronological passages in this sequence, chapters 1-2-3-4-7-8-5-6-9-10-11-12. The book of Revelation is not in Chronological order either.

Revelation should not be read numerically, in other words straight through from chapters 1 to 22. You must jump around the book Chronologically, 1-2-3-4-5-6-11-7-12-8-9-15-16-19-20-21-22. From a Chronological view point that is how you should read Revelation.

What does it mean in Daniel 12:11-12 concerning these additional days? Why are there days added to the 70th Week of Daniel's prophecy? There must be a reason for God to add these additional days to Daniel's prophecy. Daniel in verse 11 seems to refer to his prophecy in Daniel 9:27 when the Antichrist breaks his covenant that he confirmed with the Jewish people at the halfway point of the tribulation period,

"And from the time that the daily sacrifice shall be taken away, and the abomination that maketh desolate set up, there shall be a thousand two hundred and ninety days."

The Little Horn of Daniel 7:8, also known as the beast of Revelation 13:1 will put a cessation to Jewish animal sacrifice in a third rebuilt Jewish Temple. This Temple desecration will kick off the last half of Daniel's 70th Week. The last half of the tribulation is 1,260 days. The Bible breaks down this number in various ways:

Daniel 7:25- "a time and times and the dividing of time."

Daniel 12:7- "a time, times, and an half;"

Revelation 11:2- "forty and two months"

Revelation 11:3- "a thousand two hundred and threescore days"

Revelation 12:6- "a thousand two hundred and threescore days"

Revelation 12:14- "a time, and times, and half a time"

Revelation 13:5- "forty and two months"

In Daniel 12:11, Daniel says there shall be 1,290 days. So, if the last half of the tribulation period is 1,260 days, why do we have 30 days added to the 1,260 days? There must be a reason for this! We can't be dogmatic as to why the additional days. Maybe some of you can offer an explanation as to what you think as you read this. The Bible does not give us a reason as to why 30 days are added to Daniel's prophecy.

I guess we can offer a sanctified speculation as to why these additional days are giving. Daniel is talking about the Abomination of Desolation in verse 11. This goes back to Daniel 9:27. Daniel adds 30 days to this prophecy, making it 1,290 rather than 1,260. My guess is the additional 30 days are added before the Abomination of Desolation, perhaps as a 30-day announcement to the Jews of the Antichrist intentions and give the Jewish people ample time to flee before the Temple desecration.

Again, I am only offering a sanctified speculation here. At the same time the 30-days could be added at the end of the 1,260 days of the Great Tribulation, giving time for God to judge Israel and the Nations. At Jesus second coming at the end of Daniel's 70th Week He sends forth His angels to separate the saved and the lost, the sheep from the goats. The sheep, the saved of the tribulation, and the goats, the lost of the tribulation. So, you have a 30-day interval to judge Israel, the Nations of the world, and to establish Jesus Theocratic Davidic Kingdom in Jerusalem that will last for 1000 years with David's Throne reestablished.

However, when we get to Daniel 12:12 we see more days added to the 1,290 days. We now see another 45 days added to the 1,290 days. So now we have a number of 1,335 days added to the prophecy.

"Blessed is he that waiteth, and cometh to the <u>thousand three hundred and five and thirty days</u>."

Daniel tells us "Blessed" בָּרוּךְ "Baruch," simply means fortunate. Daniel tells us" blessed is he that waiteth and cometh to the thousand three hundred and five and thirty days" We have an additional 45 days beyond the figure of verse 11. The additional days probably occurs between the Great Tribulation and prior to the commencement of the Millennial Kingdom Reign of Jesus the Messiah. With Daniel using the words, "Blessed and Waiteth" should give us a heads up.

The 45-days between the end of Daniel's 70th Week and the commencement of the Kingdom would give time for, 1. Resurrection of the Old Testament Saints, (Isa 26:19; Dan 12:2), 2. The resurrection of tribulation martyred Saints, (Luke 19:12-27; Rev 20:4),3. to erect a Millennial Temple by Jesus, (Zech 6:12-13), 4. judgment of Israel and the nations, (Matt 25), 5. Satan bound in the bottomless pit, (Rev 20:1-2).

Those surviving tribulation Saints are probably waiting for all this to come to an end, and then enter the inauguration of the

Millennial Kingdom to experience the blessings of Jesus reign from Jerusalem. Again, maybe someone has another take on what they believe Daniel is referring to concerning these additional days. If you follow a proper biblical Hermeneutic I would love to listen to your take on this.

The Year of Jubilee and Israel's 70th Anniversary

Leviticus 25:8-13

8 And thou shalt number seven sabbaths of years unto thee, seven times seven years; and the space of the seven sabbaths of years shall be unto thee forty and nine years.

9 Then shalt thou cause the trumpet of the jubile to sound on the tenth [day] of the seventh month, in the day of atonement shall ye make the trumpet sound throughout all your land.

10 And ye shall hallow the fiftieth year, and proclaim liberty throughout [all] the land unto all the inhabitants thereof: it shall be a jubile unto you; and ye shall return every man unto his possession, and ye shall return every man unto his family.

11 A jubile shall that fiftieth year be unto you: ye shall not sow, neither reap that which groweth of itself in it, nor gather [the grapes] in it of thy vine undressed.

12 For it [is] the jubile; it shall be holy unto you: ye shall eat the increase thereof out of the field.

13 In the year of this jubile ye shall return every man unto his possession.

The Year of Jubilee, known in Hebrew as שנת היובל "Shanat Hyoval". The Jewish people were to count seven Sabbaths, or "Sheva Shabbatot". These are Seven Sabbaths of years. They were to count seven. he Jews are to count Seven Sabbaths of years which would equal 49 years. Seven times seven is 49. So, we see 49 years on the seventh month of Yom Kippur or Day of Atonement in the 49th year of the 7th month when they blew the Shofar.

The following year would be the fiftieth year, the Year of Jubilee. On the Fiftieth Year the Jews were to proclaim Liberty throughout the land of Israel. It would be the release of Hebrew slaves and property. This is to happen every 50 years in the ancient land of Israel. Leviticus 25 is inscribed on the American Liberty Bell in Philadelphia. Leviticus 25 prohibits anyone from selling himself or his land permanently.

The Sabbatical years every seven years is called a "Shmetah". There was to be no labor in the land during the 50th years of the Jubilee. Slaves were released, and property returned. Shofars were blasting throughout the land. The Jews were to enjoy the fruits of the land due to their labors the past six years, but on the Shmetah, the seventh year, the Sabbatical year, there is no labor, and they were to enjoy the fruit of the land.

Every man's land was to be returned with no exceptions. Slaves were to be freed and their possessions returned, whether animal, family, or wealth, all was to be returned and all were to be freed. It is the Year of Liberty. The number 50 is found some 149 times in the Bible and is related to the coming of the Holy Spirit of God. In Leviticus 23: 15 the Jews were to count 49 days or Sabbaths at the end of First fruits, on the 50th day would be the Feast of Weeks,

"And ye shall count unto you from the morrow after the sabbath, from the day that ye brought the sheaf of the wave offering; seven sabbaths shall be complete:"

The Feast of Weeks is called in Hebrew "Shavout". You better know it in the Greek as Pentecost. The 50th day would be the Feast of Pentecost. It happens 50 days after the Feast of first First fruits. We know 50 days after Jesus ascended back up into heaven in Acts 1:9, we see in Acts 2 the Promise of the Father, the coming of the Holy Spirit upon 120 Jews in Jerusalem. The number 50 represents the coming of the Holy Ghost. Acts 2:1-8 tells us,

1 And when the day of Pentecost was fully come, they were all with one accord in one place.

2 And suddenly there came a sound from heaven as of a rushing mighty wind, and it filled all the house where they were sitting.

3 And there appeared unto them cloven tongues like as of fire, and it sat upon each of them.

4 And they were all filled with the Holy Ghost, *and began to speak with other tongues, as the Spirit gave them utterance.*

5 And there were dwelling at Jerusalem Jews, devout men, out of every nation *under heaven.*

6 Now when this was noised abroad, the multitude came together, and were confounded, because that every man heard them speak in his own language.

7 And they were all amazed and marvelled, saying one to another, Behold, are not all these which speak Galilaeans?

8 And how hear we every man in our own tongue, *wherein we were born?*

These Jews from every nation came to Jerusalem to keep the three-main pilgrim feast of Passover, Pentecost, and Tabernacles. According to Deuteronomy 16:16 God required all Jews to make *Aliya* to Jerusalem for those three-main feasts. No matter where you were as a Jew, you required to be at Jerusalem. The Holy Ghost came upon 120 Jews at Jerusalem. They spoke with *other* tongues. They spoke a language not their own.

The Jews at Jerusalem who only knew Hebrew spoke in another language they were not at all familiar with. The Ruach HaKodeah, (Holy Spirit) gave them utterance, which means a spoken word, statement, or vocal sound. You had Jews from other nations who came to Jerusalem in obedience to Deuteronomy 16:16. They did not know the language of the Jews at Jerusalem, Hebrew. These Jews who lived outside the land were confused.

They were confused to the fact that they heard these Jews in Jerusalem speak their language. They knew they were Galilean

Jews and did not know their native tongue. Because of this amazing miracle, 3,000 Jews were saved, (Acts 2:41). The Jews at Jerusalem miraculously spoke a language did they did not know to communicate the gospel to the Jews living outside of Israel. Verse 8 says, *"And how hear we every man in our own tongue, wherein we were born?* Does this happen today? No. This was limited to the to the first century A.D Apostles. The Apostolic era. If I was to bring a Chinese man who knows no English into a church today who claims they speak in tongues, I guarantee you not one person who doesn't know Chinese can communicate to him in Chinese. Why? That was limited to the first century. I digress!

Just as the 50th year represents Liberty throughout the land of Israel, we have freedom from sin by the efficacious work of Jesus the Messiah on the cross, and the promise to send the Comforter who would help us along the way. God works through the number seven through the Scripture as His favorite number. The 7th day is the Shabbat, 7-Feasts of Israel (Lev 23), 70 elders of Moses, (Numbers 11:16), 70 Weeks of Prophecy (Dan 9), 7-Seals, 7-Trumpets, 7-vial judgments, twenty-one judgments in all in the book of Revelation.

The reason the Jews went into the Babylonian Captivity was because they violated the Sabbatical years. Every seven years the Shmetah was the seventh year. They were to work six years, on the 7th year the land was to have rest. So, because the Jews violated the Sabbatical years, they went in to the Babylonian captivity for a period of, 70-years. 2 Chronicles 36:21 says as long as the Jews were in the captivity, the land would enjoy her Sabbaths, her Sabbatical cycles,

"To fulfil the word of the LORD by the mouth of Jeremiah, until the land had enjoyed her sabbaths: for as long as she lay desolate she kept sabbath, to fulfil threescore and ten years."

Come May 14, 2018 would be the 70th Jubilee anniversary of the declaration of Israel's Independence. Israel was reborn on May 14, 1948, and now, we come up on the Jewish State's 70th anniversary. This will be Israel's 70th or platinum Jubilee. It was 70 years ago come May 14, 2018, Israel's first Prime Minister David Ben Gurion declared the rebirth of the State of Israel at Independence Hall in Tel Aviv.

They will hold a special ceremony at Independence Hall while they play "Ha Tikvah", (The Hope), Israel's National Anthem. An actor playing David Ben Gurion will read from the Declaration of Independence. The Jewish prophets foretold the rebirth of the State of Israel centuries ago. Isaiah 66:7-8 shows a nation born in one day, May 14, 1948. Ezekiel 37 with the Dry Bones, the regathering of the Jews back to the land.

What does all this mean as we consider biblical prophecy? What does this 70th anniversary of Israel's platinum Jubilee mean? What we know, is that the Jews are back in the land, howbeit, in unbelief. We find in Deuteronomy 4:30 that when the Jews are in the land in the latter days, the future 7-year period of tribulation is not that far off. The Jews must be in the land in unbelief in preparation for the tribulation period,

"When thou art in tribulation, and all these things are come upon thee, even in the latter days, if thou turn to the LORD thy God, and shalt be obedient unto his voice;"

We see in Daniel 9:24 that 70 weeks, or a final 7-year period will come upon Israel and their holy capitol city, the city of Jerusalem. We know that 69 of those 70 weeks have been fulfilled. One week is yet future,

"Seventy weeks are determined upon thy people and upon thy holy city, to finish the transgression, and to make an end of sins, and to make reconciliation for iniquity, and to bring in

everlasting righteousness, and to seal up the vision and prophecy, and to anoint the most Holy."

We know that "one week" is to be the final week of Daniel's 70th Week, the tribulation period. The Jews were in the 70-year captivity, Israel is about to celebrate their 70th Independence Anniversary, and, Daniel tells us in the future, the final 70th Week of Daniel's prophecy will commence. The Rapture of the church will first take place before this 70th Week of prophecy. The final 70th week of Daniel prophecy will commence sometime after the Rapture when the Antichrist confirms the covenant with Israel, (Dan 9:27),

"And he shall confirm the covenant with many for one week: and in the midst of the week he shall cause the sacrifice and the oblation to cease, and for the overspreading of abominations he shall make it desolate, even until the consummation, and that determined shall be poured upon the desolate."

We know the stage is set for these Eschatological events to happen with the Jews back in the land in preparation for these events. Israel's 70th Jubilee anniversary come May 14, 2018 reminds us the 70th Week of Daniel's prophecy is close at hand!

Are We Experiencing the Seal Judgments Now in Revelation?
Revelation 6:8

"And I looked, and behold a pale horse: and his name that sat on him was Death, and Hell followed with him. And power was given unto them over the fourth part of the earth, to kill with sword, and with hunger, and with death, and with the beasts of the earth."

Revelation 6 record the opening of the Seal judgments that commence the wrath of God being poured out on the earth during Daniel's 70th Week of prophecy. We see that the Lamb of God, Yeshua the Messiah, Jesus the Christ opens these Seals to unleash the beginning of 21 judgments that God will bring upon the rebellious sinful mankind.

God will pour twenty-one judgments on the earth, 7 Seal judgments, 7 Trumpet judgments, and 7 vial judgments. These 21 judgments will result in catastrophic events on the earth resulting in unprecedent loss of life globally. When the Lamb of God, Jesus the Messiah opens the Seals wrath it will result in the rider on a white horse, this is the Antichrist, not to be confused with the rider on the White horse in Revelation 19:11, the true Messiah, Jesus.

The opening of the second Seals results in the rider on the red horse who represents war and global conflict on the earth. This could be the result of the Ezekiel 38-39, Psalm 83, and Daniel 11:40-45 conflict. The opening of the third Seal represent famine and global starvation with the rider on the black horse. A measure of wheat for a penny, three measures of barley for a penny, and don't hurt the oil and the wine.

A penny in Roman times would be a Denarius, and it represented a day's wage. Food would be so scarce that it would have to be rationed due to a global food shortage that leads to death by starvation. The opening of the fourth Seal unleashes the pale horse who is called death with hell following him. Death takes lives and hell holds them for judgment. The pale horse kills one fourth of humanity.

We have those today in the church claiming that we are right now experiencing the Seal judgments of Revelation 6 with others claiming we are right now experiencing the Trumpet judgments of Revelation 9. How could anybody with a proper Hermeneutic even come to such a conclusion? How can anybody with a slight knowledge of Scripture anyway even think we are in the tribulation right now?

There are some prophecy teachers out there who are teaching this gross interpretation. This is due to a failure to "rightly divide the Word of truth" as read in 2 Timothy 2:15. It's a failure to rightly study Scriptures for its plain sense interpretation. Carl Gallops, a Pastor out of Milton Florida who wrote the book, "The Rabbi Who Found Messiah" believes we under the tribulation judgments right now, the Seal judgments. Another Prophecy guy on Christian TV, Irving Baxter Jr. believes we are right now experiencing the Trumpet judgments of Revelation 9. He is a Post Tribulation advocate and his Eschatology is atrocious. The people who advocate we are experiencing either the Seal wrath or Trumpet wrath judgments in the present look at the current world situation and apply certain events to what the Bible prophecy says happens in the future.

We don't look at current situations to determine what the Scriptures teach, we look at the Scriptures to determine what will happen soon, current events don't dictate Bible prophecy. The times in which we live are catching up to the Bible and not the other way around. The Bible is more up to date than tomorrow's newspaper. Do not interpret Bible prophecy to current event and say it's a fulfillment.

There are no prophecies that must be fulfilled before the Rapture. There are no signs that precede the Rapture of the church. Nothing must be fulfilled before Jesus comes to take His Bride away at the Blessed Hope. It's a shame today that the doctrine of Bible prophecy is being misused and abused by prophecy teachers. YouTube has become the platform of what I call "YouTube Eschatology". It is a platform for Prophecy sensationalist.

First, we are not in the tribulation period. How do I know that? When did Israel recently agree to a 7-year confirmation peace treaty described in Daniel 9:27? When did that happen? Not yet! It will in the future. The confirmation of the 7-year treaty between the Antichrist, the ruler of the Revived Roman Empire and Israel will begin the commencement of Daniel 70th Week of prophecy and not before. This has not happened yet.

If we are in the opening or the midst of the Seal judgments, when did one fourth of the world's population recently die? Revelation 6:8 says the rider on the pale horse takes one fourth of humanity. When did one and a half billion people recently die? Some would argue in vain that between World Wars 1 and 2 there was a staggering amount of lives lost. That is what you call a "Vexatious Argument", its full of disorder and void of common sense.

In terms of the Trumpet judgments, when did another one third of humanity perish according to Revelation 9:15 and 18? Another one and a half billion people? When did that happen? Arguing past World Wars do not cut it. And if you want to go with that fallacious argument lets go there. World War 1 resulted in 41 million deaths, including soldiers and Civilians. World War 2 was 60 million people. About 101 million totals between both wars.

That does not come even close to the numbers we find in Revelation 6:8 and 9:15 and 18. When did the earth open and unleash demonic style locust from the bottomless pit in the trumpet judgments of Revelation 9:3? That never happened! When was the Euphrates River dried up so that the kings of the east, a 200,000,000-man army crossed over? When did that happened? History or recent developments do not record any of this.

There are prophecy teachers out there who should be avoided at all cost. They are giving a gross misinterpretation of Scripture and being dramatic in their teaching. They have departed from rightly dividing the Word of truth, (2 Timothy 2:15). Recent developments are showing we are rapidly moving towards the Eschatological ramifications in the book of Revelation, but, to say we are experiencing them now is unbiblical. The Rapture is the next main event to happen before Daniel's 70th week of Prophecy.

The Wrath of God, Is it Myth or a Soon Reality?

Nahum 1:2-3; 6

2 God [is] jealous, and the LORD revengeth; the LORD revengeth, and [is] furious; the LORD will take vengeance on his adversaries, and he reserveth [wrath] for his enemies.

3 The LORD [is] slow to anger, and great in power, and will not at all acquit [the wicked]: the LORD hath his way in the whirlwind and in the storm, and the clouds [are] the dust of his feet.

"Who can stand before his indignation? and who can abide in the fierceness of his anger? his fury is poured out like fire, and the rocks are thrown down by him."

The Bible clearly describes two natures of God, Love and Wrath. Many today can accept the Love, grace, and mercy of God, but cannot comprehend the wrath of God. I am equally shocked that Christians today cannot accept a God of wrath. Satan has sold the big lie today that God is only a God of love. God will never hurt a fly. God is a big cosmic teddy bear who welcome all into heaven one day no matter what your lifestyle is what belief you have.

Satan is a murderer and a liar! He drove Cain to commit the first murder (Gen 4:8). Satan has sold the world a bill of goods concerning the two natures of God, He is a God of love, but, He is not a God of wrath. Many liberal churches today only emphasize the love of God but omit the wrath of God. You can't have one without the other. Even so with the doctrine of hell, we'll talk about heaven but uncomfortable preaching on hell. Of the 1830 verses that record the words of Jesus, 13 % of His words were on hell.

Of course, God is a God of love, John 3:16, God is love according to 1 John 4:8. The Bible strongly emphasizes the love of God. But, the Bible also strongly emphasizes the wrath of God in no uncertain terms. In terms of the love of God and the wrath of God, you can't have one without the other. Both love and wrath emphasize the two natures of God. Many today only want the love of God but not the wrath of God.

God is a God of Holiness. That holiness is undermined by the world today. That same Holiness is also undermined in the church today. We have the attitude that God winks at sin and sinful actions don't bother him. Their argument today is, remember, Jesus said turn the other cheek, (Matt 5:39). So, when it comes to sin, and sinful actions God will turn the other cheek as well. All Jesus meant was that we are not to respond to violence with violence.

In Numbers 14:18 it tells us God will deal with sin in two ways, Grace or Wrath. God is a God of love, but He will not clear the guilty who refuse to repent and will judge the iniquity of sinful men. The liberal Christian will quote John 3:16, *"For God so loved the world"*. All know that verse, even the unsaved. However, they fail to drop down twenty verses and go to John 3:36 and will not acknowledge that verse,

"He that believeth on the Son hath everlasting life: and he that believeth not the Son shall not see life; but the wrath of God abideth on him."

Romans 1:32 says God will judge those who commit the immorality of Sodomy, blasphemy, sexual immorality. We also see in 1 Corinthians 6:9 Paul the Apostle says the unrighteous shall not inherit the Kingdom of God.

Romans 1:32

"Who knowing the judgment of God, that they which commit such things are worthy of death, not only do the same, but have pleasure in them that do them."

1 Corinthians 6:9

"Know ye not that the unrighteous shall not inherit the kingdom of God? Be not deceived: neither fornicators, nor idolaters, nor adulterers, nor effeminate, nor abusers of themselves with mankind,"

We see in Ephesians 5:6 that God's wrath will come upon the children of disobedience. There will be a day of reckoning, make no mistake about it! Judgment is coming upon a sinful God hating world,

"Let no man deceive you with vain words: for because of these things cometh <u>the wrath of God</u> upon the children of disobedience."

We see in Nahum 1: 2 that God is a jealous God. The Hebrew word for Jealous is קַנּוֹא (Kahnaee), meaning He wants nothing put in front Him. He wants the preeminence in our lives, taking a back seat to no one.

We see in Nahum 1:3 that the Lord is slow to anger", Well, that would emphasize the love of God. But, when we drop down to verse 6 it says, *"who can stand before His indignation? And who can abide in the fierceness of His wrath?* The Jewish prophet Nahum presents to us the two natures of God, in verse 3 the love of God, (slow to anger), and in verse 6 the wrath of God, (His indignation). You can't have one without the other.

To leave out one without the other is unbiblical. God's two natures is Love and wrath. Don't just preach one nature, you must preach both. To leave out either one is a disservice to the Word of God. We have this unbiblical doctrine that a lot of Pastors are falling for that the wrath of God was the Old Testament God, but, the love of God is the New Testament God. They are guilty of Polytheism. They are promoting a belief system of many gods. Mormonism is a cult that promotes the belief in many gods.

The God of the New Testament is the God of the Old Testament. There are not two distinct God's of either Testament. He is the One true God. These same Pastors say the Old Testament God was a God of wrath, the New Testament God is a God of love. This is wrong! This is unbiblical! We read in Malachi 3:6 that God is immutable. His nature is immutable. The Jewish prophet Malachi emphasizes that very fact. These liberal Pastors today ignore this very passage.

"For I am the LORD, I change not; therefore ye sons of Jacob are not consumed." Yet, the writer of Hebrews says, *"Jesus Christ the same yesterday, and today, and forever,* (Heb 13:8).

In the book of Revelation, we see God pouring out His wrath on mankind during the tribulation period. God will pour out 7 Seals, 7 Trumpets, and 7 Vials upon wicked humanity. Twenty-one judgments in all. We see in Revelation 6:8 that one fourth of humanity is wiped out, in today's standards, that is one and a half billion. We see in Revelation 9: 15 and 18 another one third of humanity is killed during the trumpet judgments, another one and a half billion.

We look at Revelation 6:16-17 that the men of the earth seek shelter to try to hide from the wrath of God. They are calling for the mountains and rocks to hide them from the wrath of God the Father and God the Son,

16 And said to the mountains and rocks, Fall on us, and hide us from the face of him that sitteth on the throne, and from the wrath of the Lamb:

17 For the great day of his wrath is come; and who shall be able to stand?

The wrath of God has finally come upon humanity and the godless Governments of the world. The Bible says the great day of His wrath is come, whose wrath? Back up to verse 16, the wrath of Him who sits on the Throne and the wrath of the Lamb. If you are involved in a church that fails to preach both natures of God, a church that fails to preach on hell, a church that fails to preach Bible prophecy, get out! Go to a Bible believing church that preaches all of that.

Jesus is coming soon and it maybe today. The Rapture is the next event to happen. The world is in for a nightmare. Let's win souls and proclaim the love of God, but also warn that rejecting that love will result in the wrath of God.

What Is the Significance of The Second and Third Watch in Judaism?

Luke 12: 38-40

38 And if he shall come in the second watch, or come in the third watch, and find [them] so, blessed are those servants.

39 And this know, that if the goodman of the house had known what hour the thief would come, he would have watched, and not have suffered his house to be broken through.

40 Be ye therefore ready also: for the Son of man cometh at an hour when ye think not.

Jesus describes the day in which He will return to earth. We know that His coming will be in two stages, the first stage is the Rapture of the church which is an imminent event that can happen without any signs preceding it. The second stage will be His second coming back to earth riding on a White Horse described in Revelation 19:11. Daniel's 70th Week of Prophecy separates both these events, or better known as the 7-year tribulation.

Paul the Apostle in Titus 2:13 differentiates between both these comings. His coming for the church, and, the second coming with His church. Therefore, we differentiate between both these comings.

1. Titus 2:13 tells us:

"Looking for that blessed hope, and the glorious appearing of the great God and our Saviour Jesus Christ;"

The Blessed Hope is Jesus coming for His church at the Rapture. The Blessed Hope is when the church meets the Lord Jesus in the air. The dead in Christ and the living in Christ at that time will meet the Lord in the air. The Glorious Appearing will be Jesus Second coming back to earth at the end of the tribulation period with His Bride he snatched 7-years earlier. The army in heaven is the Bride of Messiah returning with Him.

Jesus in Luke 12:38 says if He shall come in the second watch or the third watch. Is he giving indication that he might possibly return during one of those times? We don't know! Jesus never mentions the First watch. What was the First, the Second, and the Third watch? The Jews divided the night into three watches, the first, second, and the third. The second and the third watches would be the latest hours of the night.

We see a case in point in Judges 7:19 that Gideon was a Judge in Israel and led a campaign against the occupation of the Midianites, who were oppressing the Jews at this time. Gideon came at them at night.

Gideon and the Israelites came out against the Midianites at the beginning of the "Middle Watch". This would be the second watch. The second watch would be from 9 PM to 12 AM. Gideon would have attacked the Midianites during this time. The night watches in the Bible would go this way. From 6 PM to 9 PM would be the First Watch. The Second Watch would be from 9 PM to 12 AM midnight. The Third Watch would be from 12 AM to 3 AM. The fourth watch would be from 3 AM to 6 AM.

Psalm 63:6 talks about lying in bed and meditate on God during the night watches. Jesus describes the night watches concerning His return in Mark 13: 35-37, He tells us to "watch" for His return;

35 Watch ye therefore: for ye know not when the master of the house cometh, at even, or at midnight, or at the cockcrowing, or in the morning:

36 Lest coming suddenly he find you sleeping.

37 And what I say unto you I say unto all, Watch.

Again, in Luke 12:38 Jesus mentioned the second watch (9 AM to 12 AM) and the third watch (12 AM to 3 AM). But Jesus never mentioned the first watch (6 PM to 9 PM). He likens His return to the 2nd or 3rd watch. He does make mention to the first watch in Mark 13:35 as "at evening" (6 PM to 9 PM). But in Luke 12:38 Jesus omits the first watch. In Revelation 2-3 we have 7 messages to seven historical churches from Jesus.

The first three churches, Ephesus, Smyrna, and Pergamos, there is no mention by Jesus of His coming to those three churches. His message to those churches do not contain any reference to His coming. These 3 churches marked the early days of the church from the Apostles down to the reign of Constantine, who legalized Christianity and Christianized the Roman Empire and ceased Christian persecution.

During this period of these 3 churches we have the first watch or "even" (Mk 13:35). In Luke 12:38 Jesus does not mention the first watch. The next 4 churches, Thyatira, Sardis, Philadelphia, and Laodicea, Jesus makes mention of His return.

It seems to me that these four churches and the attitudes they have are indicative of many churches today who operate simultaneously on earth until the Lord calls His Bride to Glory at the Rapture. The first 3 churches, history, no mention of his coming, the last 4 churches, future, He makes mention of His coming.

With the rise of Thyatira, we see the development of Catholicism and the dark ages. Later during the dark ages Protestantism arises represented by Sardis, cold, and dead. Very indifferent. Catholicism and Protestantism combined was dark, the second watch.

During the dark ages they lost interest in the coming of the Lord. In the 19th century the coming of the Lord gained more interest. In Matthew 25:6 it says, "At midnight a cry was made". The awakening of prophecy with the church of Philadelphia.

Philadelphia was faithful to the Word of God. Finally, there is Laodicea, the Lukewarm you make me sick church. The last four churches would represent the third watch, with a mixture of faithful believers and Lukewarm professing Christianity. Jesus said when He returns will He find faith on the earth? (Luke 18:8). Jesus said He will avenge speedily. He will separate the sheep from the goats. The saved from the lost when He comes. When will the Lord return? At evening? Midnight? or morning? I believe Jesus is going by Jewish time here. The Jewish day begins at evening and ends at evening, the evening and the morning were a full day in the Scripture, (Gen 1:5; 1:8; 1:13; 1:19; 1:23; 1:31).

When will Jesus return? The first, second, or third watch? We don't know! When He does come it will be daylight on one side of earth and nighttime on the other side, (Luke 17:34-35), this is true of the Rapture and second coming. We are told by Paul prior to the Rapture that we are to be children of light and not darkness. We are not to be spiritually dead in doctrine or works, but we are to watch and be sober. We see in 1 Thessalonians 5: 1-9,

1 But of the times and the seasons, brethren, ye have no need that I write unto you.

2 For yourselves know perfectly that the day of the Lord so cometh as a thief in the night.

3 For when they shall say, Peace and safety; then sudden destruction cometh upon them, as travail upon a woman with child; and they shall not escape.

4 But ye, brethren, are not in darkness, that that day should overtake you as a thief.

5 Ye are all the children of light, and the children of the day: we are not of the night, nor of darkness.

6 Therefore let us not sleep, as [do] others; but let us watch and be sober.

7 For they that sleep sleep in the night; and they that be drunken are drunken in the night.

8 But let us, who are of the day, be sober, putting on the breastplate of faith and love; and for an helmet, the hope of salvation.

9 For God hath not appointed us to wrath, but to obtain salvation by our Lord Jesus Christ,

It's getting late and the hour is at hand for Jesus soon coming. Will He come in the second or third watch? He does not mention the first watch in Luke 12:38. We don't know for sure why he does not mention the first watch. All we know is that He will call us home soon at the Rapture!

83

Notes

The Menorah and The Son of Man in the Midst of the Candlesticks
Revelation 1:12-13

12 And I turned to see the voice that spake with me. And being turned, I saw seven golden candlesticks;

13 And in the midst of the seven candlesticks [one] like unto the Son of man, clothed with a garment down to the foot, and girt about the paps with a golden girdle.

In Revelation 1:12-16 we have the only snapshot of Jesus in the Bible. It is the only description we have of Him in the Scriptures. John the Apostle sees the Son of Man in all His Glory in heaven. 1. Jesus is in the midst of the seven candlesticks. He is called the Son of man. He is called the Son of man some 79 times in the New Testament. Ezekiel is called son of man some 92 times in his Apocalyptic book. It is a Messianic title of Jesus in Daniel 7:13,

"I saw in the night visions, and, behold, one like the Son of man came with the clouds of heaven, and came to the Ancient of days, and they brought him near before him."

The number Seven is replete in the Word of God. It is God's favorite number in the Bible. It is the number of perfection, the number of completion. God created the world in 7 days, God gave Israel 7 feast, God chose 70 elders to assist Moses, Joshua and Israel marched around Jericho 7 times on the 7th day.

The number 7 is replete in the book of Revelation, 7 candlesticks, 7 churches, 7 Seals, 7 trumpets, 7 Vial judgments. A future 7-year period of tribulation to come. The Rabbis tell us humanity would go on for 6,000 years and then a 7th year of rest, the Messianic Kingdom. The Davidic Theocratic Reign of Messiah from Jerusalem.

What are these Candlesticks that Jesus the Son of man is in the midst of? When you read the Bible with Jewish eyes and understand the Jewish character of the Scriptures you would know exactly what they are. This would be the Menorah. The Menorah is a seven-branched candelabra that gave light in the Tabernacle and the first and second Jewish Temples. It would be lit daily by the High Priest, the Cohen Hagadol, with fresh oil.

Menorah outside the Temple Institute in Jerusalem

We find the description of the Menorah or candlestick in the book of Exodus 25:31-40. It was made of pure gold. We see in verse 37 that it has seven lamps or knobs to give light to the Tabernacle of Testimony. The knobs held the pure olive oil, שמן זית "Shemen Zeit". It was replaced daily by the Cohen HaGadol, the Jewish High Priest.

Three branches on either side with a middle knob that would make seven in all. Verse 39 reminds us that it was made with pure gold. The Temple Institute in Jerusalem has a replica of the Menorah constructed according to Archaeological evidence and Halachic Law.

We see another reference to the Menorah in Scripture in Zechariah 4:2 where the Jewish prophet sees a candlestick or lampstand made of gold with seven lamps with a bowl on the top of it,

"And said unto me, What seest thou? And I said, I have looked, and behold <u>a candlestick all of gold</u>, with a bowl upon the top of it, and his <u>seven lamps</u> thereon, and <u>seven pipes</u> to the <u>seven lamps</u>, which are upon the top thereof:"

1. This sounds much like a Menorah. Another Jewish lampstand is called a "Hannukiah". It is used for the Jewish holiday of Hanukkah. There is a difference between the Menorah with seven branches and a Hanukkiah with eight branches and a top branch called in Hebrew a "Servant" or Shammash in Hebrew.

The Hanukkiah has a top branch which is called in Hebrew a "Shamash" branch or servant branch. The servant branch lights the eight branches, once per night for the next eight nights of Hanukkah. What did Jesus say of Himself in Matthew 20:28? The Son of Man came not to be ministered unto, but to minister. He came to serve, not to be served. The top branch of the Hanukkiah gives light to the eight branches. Yeshua said "Ani Or, Ha, Olam", which is Hebrew for, "I am the light of the world". Now that the light of the world is in heaven, Jesus has called you and I to be a light to the world, (Matt 5:16).

 This commemorates the Maccabean victory over the Seleucid Greeks and Antiochus Epiphanes, and the one-day supply oil found in the Temple that burned miraculously for eight days. The miracle of Hanukkah. Hanukkah is known as the Festival of Lights or the Feast of the Dedication. We find one reference to this holiday in the Gospel of John 10:22 where Jesus is in Jerusalem as a Jew, a Rabbi celebrating this feast.

1. We read in John 10:22-23;

"22 And it was at Jerusalem the feast of the dedication, and it was winter." 23 And Jesus walked in the temple in Solomon's porch".

We see in the book of Revelation these seven Menorahs and Jesus in the very middle of these Menorahs. Jesus is in the very midst of these Candlesticks. But, what do these Menorahs or candlesticks represent? The Bible is its best own interpreter when we take the Scriptures for their plain sense interpretation. We compare Scripture with Scripture to ascertain more information concerning a person, place, or thing.

We will apply Inductive Bible Study and show how the Scriptures interpret themselves. We will Exegete the Scriptures to draw the meaning out of the text. We will avoid Eisegeses, to put one's own ideas into the text. This is a major problem in the church today with Christians who Eisegeses as a form of biblical interpretation. This is wrong. We are bringing our own thoughts and ideas to the table, and we determine what the text ought to say.

In Revelation 1:12-13, we see Jesus in the midst of the candlesticks. What do the candlesticks represent? In verse 16 we see seven stars in Jesus right hand. What do the 7 stars represent? This is where Indictive Bible study comes into play. It is a very rich approach to biblical Hermeneutics, the Science of Bible interpretation. You will see how the Bible itself will interpret verses 12 and 16. Revelation 1:20 gives us the interpretation of verses 12 and 16. Not me or anyone else, but the Word of God alone,

"The mystery of the seven stars which thou sawest in my right hand, and the seven golden candlesticks. The seven stars are the angels of the seven churches: and the seven candlesticks which thou sawest are the seven churches."

The seven stars are the angels of the seven churches and the seven candlesticks or Menorahs are the seven churches. These angels are not human beings or Pastors of these seven churches. They are angels. If the Bible says angels, they are angels. We know they are angels because we find the Greek word *"angelos"*. If they were humans or Pastors, we would find the Greek word *"poiman"*. Poiman is the Greek word for Pastor. We don't find that here.

 The Son of man, Yeshua the Messiah will one day come to take his Church home. He is in the midst of His True Bible believing blood washed church now. His church began 2,000 years ago at Pentecost in Jerusalem. Jesus some 2,000 years ago said, "Ani Or, Ha, Olam" I am the Light of the World. In Matthew 5:16 He calls us to be a light to the world, to those who are in darkness to bring them to the light of the Messiah, both Jew and Gentile.

 The Menorah gave light to the Tabernacle and the first and second Jewish Temples. The Hanukkiah gives light for the eight days of the observance of Hanukkah. Christmas corresponds to Hanukkiah because of the lights in December. I happen to be in Israel in 2016 for Hanukkah, and had the opportunity to go to Modin, an ancient town half way between Tel Aviv and

Jerusalem where the Macabees are buried. Where the Hanukkah story begins.

Both Hanukkah and Christmas take place in the winter in the Jewish month Kislev, corresponding to the month of December. Both holidays deal with burning lights. We are to be light 365 days a year to a wicked dark an evil world in which we live. The Light of the world, the Son of man is coming soon in this event we call the Rapture which could happen at any moment! Come soon Lord Jesus! Maranatha!

Notes

Ancient Jewish Wedding Customs and John 14:1-3

1 Let not your heart be troubled: ye believe in God, believe also in me.

2 In my Father's house are many mansions: if [it were] not [so], I would have told you. I go to prepare a place for you.

3 And if I go and prepare a place for you, I will come again, and receive you unto myself; that where I am, [there] ye may be also.

In biblical times, people were married in early youth, and marriages were usually contracted within the narrow circle of the clan and the Jewish family. As a rule, the fathers arranged the match. The girl was consulted, but the calling of the damsel and inquiring at her mouth, she made the final call.

In those days a father was more concerned about the marriage of his sons than about the marriage of his daughters. No expense was involved in marrying off a daughter. The father received a dowry for his daughter whereas he had to give a dowry to the prospective father-in-law of his son when marrying him off.

The price paid by the father of the groom to the father of the bride was called the mohar. The term continues to be included in the text of the traditional ketubah, or Jewish wedding contract. In Genesis 34:12 we see Dinah being purchased by Shechem, a Hivite to have her after he had defiled her. This did not sit well with her brothers Simeon and Levi and killed the men that defiled her.

A "Dowry" simply means, property or money brought by a bride to her husband on their marriage. In this case Abba, the Dad would pay for the bride for his son. "Mattana" was the Hebrew word for the gifts, given by the groom to the bride in addition to the mohar, the cash that was paid.

The mohar was not always paid in cash. Sometimes it was paid in kind, or in service. The Book of Genesis relates the story of the servant of Abraham. His request for Rebecca [to marry Isaac] was granted, "she was brought forth jewels of silver, and jewels of gold, and raiment, and gave them for Rebecca.

The mohar was originally the purchase price of the bride, and it is therefore understandable why it was paid by the father of the groom to the father of the bride. In ancient days, marriage was not an agreement between two individuals, but between two families. The newly married man usually did not find a new home for himself but occupied a nook in his father's house.

First came the betrothal [erusin]; and later, the wedding [nissuin]. At the betrothal the woman was legally married, although she still remained in her father's house. She could not belong to another man unless she was divorced from her betrothed. The wedding meant only that the betrothed woman, accompanied by a colorful procession, was brought from her father's house to the house of her groom's father, and the legal tie with him was consummated.

Marriage, as with any type of purchase, consisted of two acts. First the price was paid, and an agreement reached on the conditions of sale. The mohar was paid and a detailed agreement reached between the families of the bride and groom.

This betrothal was followed by the wedding, when the bride was brought into the home of the groom, who took actual possession of her. They would go to Groom's Father's house to Consummate the marriage. This honey moon would last for seven days. At the seventh day the Jewish Groom and Bride would have the feast for the Wedding Guest. Today in Israel they still have a seven-day celebration.

Jesus in John 14 the night before His crucifixion beautifully displays the Jewish Wedding Customs. He left His Father's House in Heaven. He paid the price for His Bride, the Church when He shed His blood. He sealed the Wedding contract by His blood and went back to His Father's House. He promised His

Bride He would return and bring her back with Him to His Father's House. She is waiting for His return.

He will return and take us to heaven where we will be with Him for seven years, after the seven years there will be a great feast in heaven at the marriage supper of the Lamb in Revelation 19:7-9,

7 Let us be glad and rejoice, and give honour to him: for the marriage of the Lamb is come, and his wife hath made herself ready.

8 And to her was granted that she should be arrayed in fine linen, clean and white: for the fine linen is the righteousness of saints.

9 And he saith unto me, Write, Blessed [are] they which are called unto the marriage supper of the Lamb. And he saith unto me, These are the true sayings of God.

We will than mount on White horses and come back to earth with our Groom, the Lamb of God, and He will establish His Kingdom for one thousand years. His Bride will be at His side. We are right now in the Betrothal stage, the church age, as we wait for our Groom to return. The Betrothal stage only lasted a year, it was very brief before the Wedding and Marriage supper.

The church age began at Pentecost and we have been in that age for 2,000 years. The church age is about to end when the Rapture takes place. We will go to the Father's House for 7-years to consummate the marriage. At the end of the 7-years we will have such a great Wedding Feast, we will have invited guest, that will be Israel, at the marriage supper. Saved Israel of the tribulation that was not part of the church age.

The ancient Jewish wedding customs of 2,000 years ago are still being practiced in Israel today. Jesus will fulfill the Jewish Wedding customs when He comes for His Bride He paid the price for, the Church. He Will Rapture His church home soon!

Notes

Why the Pre-Tribulation Rapture?

Revelation 3:10

"Because thou hast kept the word of my patience, I also will keep thee from the hour of temptation, which shall come upon all the world, to try them that dwell upon the earth."

One of the most attacked positions in terms of Eschatology is the doctrine of the Pre-Tribulation Rapture position. Not only is this position attacked, the doctrine of the Rapture itself is under attack.

There are many Christians today who now reject the doctrine of the Rapture as an unbiblical doctrine that should not be taught in the church because the word Rapture is not found in the Scriptures.

All because a word is not found in Scripture does not mean the doctrine connected to that word is not there. I think it's disingenuous to say that a doctrine does not exist in the Bible because a certain word is not found.

Words like the Trinity, Demons, Bible, Rapture, Missions, or Missionary, do not appear in the Word of God, but that does not mean the doctrines connected to these words do not appear. It's a straw-man argument to argue otherwise.

I preached at a Messianic Jewish Congregation in Indiana a few years back on a Saturday morning and some Christians refused to come out because they heard I was teaching on the doctrine of the Rapture.

The doctrine of the Rapture is slowly dying in our churches. Christians today are no longer yearning for the Lord's return, but we are now yawning about the Lord's return. It's a Laodicean attitude concerning Bible prophecy.

One third of the Bible deals with Bible prophecy. Prophecy takes up about 33% of the Word of God. From the book of Daniel chapter 1 to the book of Revelation chapter 22 is about 33% of Scripture.

One out of every three pages of the Scriptures deal with the subject of Bible prophecy. From Daniel to Revelation is about 400 of the 1189 chapters that deal with the subject of Eschatology, the doctrine of last things.

It's unfortunate today that many Pastors are robbing their congregation of the doctrine of the Blessed Hope by failing to, or at least occasionally teach prophecy. Christians are ignoring the matter or simply refusing to believe it.

If one third of the Bible is Eschatological, if 33% of the Scriptures are prophetic, if we have 400 of the 1189 chapters that deal with prophecy, wouldn't you say the subject is important to God? Why not to us?

Some in the church would say, well, let's leave prophecy alone and let God deal with it. It is not for us to know about such things. It's too deep a study and too controversial so just leave it alone. Keep prophecy where it belongs, the future.

Some would use Jesus words in Acts 1:7 *"It is not for you to know the times or the seasons, which the Father hath put in his own power."* Jesus was referring to the coming of the Messianic Kingdom the Jews wanted immediately! It's not a passage to discourage the study of Bible prophecy and should not be used as such.

Revelation 1:3 tells us that we are to study this precious subject. We are to read Scripture concerning this doctrine of the Blessed Hope. Nowhere in the Bible are we told to ignore the subject, nowhere!

"Blessed is he that readeth, and they that hear the words of this prophecy, and keep those things which are written therein: for the time is at hand."

So, we have key words here, *blessed, read, hear,* and *keep.* *Blessed* means fortunate, reading is a way of obtaining information through your eye gate, hearing, is when you hear the subject taught and preached (Rom 10:17), and keep, you hide it in your heart, (Psalm 119:11).

Why do we believe in the doctrine of the Pre-tribulation Rapture? Despite many differing views out there in the church, we believe the best position is the Pre-Tribulation view based on the literal plain sense interpretation of Scripture.

I want to show proof text that clearly show the church will not be present on the earth during the 70th Week of Daniel's prophecy, or 7-year period of tribulation to come upon sinful rebellious humanity.

We read in Jeremiah 30: 7 concerning this future period. The tribulation is also called, 'the time of Jacob's trouble". Jacob is Israel based on Genesis 32:28, a time of Israel's trouble, a time of distress,

"Alas! for that day is great, so that none is like it: it is even the time of Jacob's trouble; but he shall be saved out of it."

We see in Daniel 9:24 that *"Seventy Weeks"* are determined upon *thy people,* and *thy holy city.* What people? Christians or Jews? Obviously, Jews because the holy city is the city of Jerusalem, Israel's capitol.

In Daniel 12:1 he says that in the future Michael the Archangel will fight on behalf of a certain people in the tribulation period, which people? The children of thy people, (Jews) during a time of trouble, Jacob's trouble,

"And at that time shall Michael stand up, the great prince which standeth for the <u>children of thy people</u>: and there shall be <u>a time of trouble,</u> such as never was since there was a nation even to

that same time: and at that time thy people shall be delivered, every one that shall be found written in the book."

Once again, Inductive Bible study comes into play here. The parallel passage to Daniel 12:1 concerning Michael standing up for the Jews in the tribulation is Revelation 12:7-9. Michael defeats the Dragon, Satan, in his quest to kill the Jews,

7 And there was war in heaven: Michael and his angels fought against the dragon; and the dragon fought and his angels,

8 And prevailed not; neither was their place found any more in heaven.

9 And the great dragon was cast out, that old serpent, called the Devil, and Satan, which deceiveth the whole world: he was cast out into the earth, and his angels were cast out with him.

We see other passages in the New Testament that strongly imply the church will not go through any of the tribulation period. It's a time of Jacob's trouble, not the churches trouble. The church was not in the 69th week of prophecy, nor, will the church be in the 70th week.

1. We see in Romans 5:9

"Much more then, being now justified by his blood, we shall be saved from wrath through him."

1 Thessalonians 1:10

"And to wait for his Son from heaven, whom he raised from the dead, even Jesus, which delivered us from the wrath to come."

1 Thessalonians 5:9

"*For God hath not appointed us to wrath,* but to obtain salvation by our Lord Jesus Christ,"

Revelation 3:10

"*Because thou hast kept the word of my patience, I also will keep thee from the hour of temptation, which shall come upon all the world,* to try them that dwell upon the earth.

The book of Revelation itself is proof in the pudding the church will not be on the earth in the tribulation. We see the church mentioned 25 times in Revelation before and after the tribulation.

We see the church mentioned 19 times before Revelation 4:1 and mentioned 6 times after Revelation 19:11. The church is never mentioned as being on earth between those 16 chapters that cover the tribulation period.

Why would God save us from going to hell, but, beat us up in the tribulation makes no sense at all! Some in the church claim the church must go through the tribulation period to be purified. That is just nonsense!

By making an absurd statement like that your guilty of creating a Protestant Purgatory. That is just outright hubris! The church has been purified by the blood of the Lamb, not by the 70th week, that's ridiculous!

Christians can rest assure we can take God at His Word that Jesus promised to take us home before these apocalyptic events occur. That's why Jesus said, "*Let not your heart be troubled*" (John 14:1). Paul in the great Rapture passage said, "*Comfort one another with these words*" (1 Thess 4:18).

101

Notes

102

Notes

Mockers Mocking the Rapture

2 Peter 3:3-4

3 Knowing this first, that there shall come in the last days scoffers, walking after their own lusts,

4 And saying, Where is the promise of his coming? for since the fathers fell asleep, all things continue as [they were] from the beginning of the creation.

The Apostle Peter describes a last day's scenario of those who would deny the promise of the Blessed Hope. They will refuse to believe the fact that Jesus is about to return to call His Bride Home.

Peter further warns that in the last days of the church age there would be *"Scoffers"* literally, mockers who will ridicule the promise that Jesus is coming again. They will mock the idea of His soon return.

The last days began with the birth of Jesus the Messiah in Bethlehem. His birth initiated the last days. We have been in the last days for nearly 2,000 years. The church age began at Pentecost in Acts 2.

We have had 2,000 years of church age history from Pentecost until now. The church age will come to an end at the Rapture of the church. The coming of Jesus to remove His church will end the current church age.

What is really disturbing, is that most of this mocking at the idea of Jesus return at the Rapture is taken place in the church. The majority of this mockery is coming from within the church.

A few years back, the Times of Israel reported that a high-ranking Bishop at the Vatican declared that after 2,000 years they will no longer wait for Jesus return. When asked why he said, "turning water into wine has it's up and downs, we all make promises we can't keep when we are drunk, and Jesus was no different".

Those within the church are calling God a liar when they deny that Jesus is coming back. They are walking in their own fleshly desires in seeking to persuade others to drop this notion of the Rapture.

Facebook has become a stomping ground for doctrinal wars among Christians. Even Pastors that I know personally are causing controversy and even promoting some heretical thoughts on simple truth doctrine.

I frankly find this absolutely disgusting! These Pastors could be in study, preparing their sermons, in prayer, or using social media to win souls and promote their church. Instead, they make social media into an all-out free for all doctrinal war with nasty name calling.

I am appalled to see how Christians are conducting themselves on Facebook. Trashing other believers, trashing other churches and even attacking their own church and Pastor publicly because of a disagreement. This is what it has come to?

These mockers will argue as Peter predicted in 2 Peter 3:4, "And, saying, Where is the promise of His coming?". The straw-man argument among these mockers is that we have been preaching Jesus return for 2,000 years. He has not returned, so He is not coming back.

It's been 2,000 years. Why hasn't He returned? The world grows worse. Evil abounds. Apostasy has plagued the church by and large. Wars taking place and terrorism globally. And look! He has not returned.

So, according to these mockers, this means Jesus is not coming back. After all that has taken place in the world Jesus should have returned by now, He hasn't! So, that means He will not come back. This is a futile argument at best to deny His soon coming.

Peter goes on to tell us, *"for since the father fell asleep, all things continue as they were from the beginning of the creation"*. See, since the beginning you been proclaiming this promise of His coming and He has not come.

Again, let me reiterate, most of this mocking of the Rapture, the mockery of Jesus soon coming is from those within the church. The doctrine of the Rapture is ridiculed, especially the Pre-Tribulation Rapture view as we discussed in the last chapter.

To deny that Jesus is coming back makes you a liar, and even worse, makes God a liar. Romans 3:4 says *let God be true, but every man a liar*. God's Word is absolute. It is true from the very beginning.

It is man that contradicts God's Word. It is man who lies and manipulates. It is man who adds and subtracts from God's Word. It is man who makes God out to be some type of heavenly cosmic monster.

When Paul says let God be true but every man a liar, that goes for those within and outside the church. God never intended his church to act in this form or manner. And yet, on Facebook I cringe at the behavior of Christians, even more so, Pastors.

2 Peter chapter 3 in context is living in the hope of the Lord's return. Peter is defending the fact that Jesus will return as He has promised. He is encouraging his readers to ignore the mockers and rest on the promises of God.

What really amazes me is that 2 Peter 3:5 tells us they see the evidence of Jesus coming in the Scriptures, but, still deny He will return. In other words, they are stuck on stupid! They willingly enjoy walking in their own lust,

"For this they willingly are ignorant of, that by the word of God the heavens were of old, and the earth standing out of the water and in the water:"

They will deny creation, they will deny a global flood, they will deny the inerrancy of God's Word, they will deny Jesus deity, and yes, they will deny the coming of Christ. Believe it or not, these doctrines are even debated among Christians.

We see another parallel verse to 2 Peter 3:3-4 in Jude 18. Like Peter, Jude ridicules these mockers who deny that Jesus is coming back. Peter and Jude go after apostates, false teachers, and Christ deniers,

18 How that they told you there should be mockers in the last time, who should walk after their own ungodly lusts.

Jude, like Peter uses the phrase, *"last time"* or *last days*. In the last days these mockers will walk in their own ungodly lust. They seek to argue, debate, feed their own ego to fulfill their lust. They are out to prove you wrong to feed their flesh.

I have been cursed at by so-called Christians, I have been ostracized on Facebook because I stood up against this mockery within the church. Facebook has become an unpleasant place to be because of Christian doctrinal wars.

Jesus is coming back! Take God at His Word on this. It does not matter what man says or even those in the church. We must take God at His promises. We must believe every jot and tittle of His Word.

Conditions are unfolding exponentially worldwide signaling that Jesus is coming soon. No signs or prophecies precede the Rapture, that event is imminent. The Rapture is the next main event. It will happen, you can count on it!

Notes

Jesus: The Name Above Every Name
Philippians 2:6-11

6 Who, being in the form of God, thought it not robbery to be equal with God:

7 But made himself of no reputation, and took upon him the form of a servant, and was made in the likeness of men:

8 And being found in fashion as a man, he humbled himself, and became obedient unto death, even the death of the cross.

9 Wherefore God also hath highly exalted him, and given him a name which is above every name:

10 That at the name of Jesus every knee should bow, of things in heaven, and things in earth, and things under the earth;

11 And that every tongue should confess that Jesus Christ is Lord, to the glory of God the Father.

The Name of Jesus is above every name. He is the son of the living God. He walked this earth 2,000 years ago as God Almighty in human flesh, the Creator of heaven and earth. He is perfect without sin.

 No one can come close to the person of Jesus in terms of being perfect. No one is on the same level as the Son of God. Jesus is in a class of His own as the perfect sinless Son of Man who became the unblemished sacrifice for sinful men.

 Jesus was born of a Virgin, born without the taint of original sin, defied death by rising from the dead. He is now seated at the right hand of the Father and has promised to return with power and glory.

The Name of Jesus is known globally. His Name triggers emotions when mentioned, whether positively or negatively. Just the mention of His Name makes the demons tremble. There is power in that Name.

Paul says in Philippians 2 that Jesus was in the form of God. It's like looking in the mirror and seeing your form. When you look at Jesus you look at God Himself. He was equal with God as the second person of the Triune Godhead, or what we call the Trinity.

He did not come to earth 2,000 years ago make any reputation, in other words Jesus came to serve, not to be served. He took the form of a servant as God in human form. Galatians 4:4 tells us God sent His Son born of a woman.

As a man, as God in human form Jesus humbled Himself. He was obedient to the Father. Jesus emptied Himself when He made Himself of no reputation. In other words, He veiled His Very Glory.

This is where we get the Greek word *Kenosis*, which means "emptying". Jesus emptied Himself by veiling His Glory, taking on Himself a true but sinless human nature, and voluntarily submitting to the will of the Father.

The only time we see Jesus in the Synoptic Gospels unveil His Glory during his public ministry on earth is at the Transfiguration in Matthew 17 where we believed this took place on Mt. Hermon on the Golan Heights in Israel.

Jesus was transfigured, the verb is the Greek *"metamorphoo"*, a transformation of essential form proceeding from within. There is a spiritual *metamorphoo,* a metamorphosis when you and I got saved, (2 Cor 5:17; Rom 12:2).

Jesus remained God, retaining the nature and attributes of God, but, taking a sinless human nature to have a ministry among sinful men. To preach the Gospel of the Kingdom, calling on men to repent, for the Kingdom of heaven is at hand.

We today as the body of Messiah 2,000 years later must preach the gospel. We must preach repentance, and faith in Jesus as

Lord and personal Savior. There are too many false gospels out there.

Today the Cults are propagating a false Jesus. They don't have the Jesus of the Bible. They have re-created a false Jesus who is nothing but a mortal man like you and me. To them Jesus was just a good man, but not God in the flesh.

Today the Cults deny the deity of Jesus. They say He was not God, He is Michael the Archangel as the Jehovah's Witnesses cult present Him. Other say Jesus was the brother of Lucifer and just an exalted man like the Mormons. They have the wrong Jesus.

Do an experiment on Google. Google the name of Mohammed, the founder of Islam who has been dead for nearly 1500 years. You will get 49,500,000 hits on Google. Mohammed died June 8 632 A.D.

Now, Google the Name of Jesus. I did, and I came up with 289,000,000 hits on the Google search engine. Jesus is more known and revered then Mohammed. Jesus was born in Bethlehem of Judea, died around 32 A.D. But, what separates Jesus from Mohammed is that Jesus rose from the dead. Mohammed did not.

So, who is Jesus? I found 289,000,000 hits for Jesus on Google. But, if you have a Google Home device, and you ask that device who is Jesus Christ? Google Home will tell you, "I have no clue". Really?

I have an Amazon Echo dot. I asked Alexa, who is Jesus Christ? Alexa responded by saying, "Jesus Christ is the Son of God who walked this earth 2,000 years ago". So, what is Google's problem with Jesus?

Some say that the Google Home device has an aversion to Christianity. Google Home can tell you who Mohammed is, who Buddha is, who Allah is, who Confucius is, but, have no clue who Jesus is?

When you ask Google Home who Jesus Christ is, the reply you get is, "Sorry, I don't know how to help with that". Does Google have a problem with Jesus Christ? Google Home can't tell you who God is either.

I think something sinister is at play here. I believe Google has taken God and Jesus Christ out of the smart audio. It started with Schools and now with home devices. We don't want to offend anyone today. Again, the mention of Jesus Name stirs emotion in people. There is power in that Name!

Google released a statement to Fox saying, "It meant no disrespect to Christians or the Son of God". Of course, you meant disrespect! Google wants to be politically correct and not offend the Jesus haters.

Hey Google, who is Jesus? He is the Son of God, the risen Savior, the Creator of heaven and earth. Anyone who calls on His Name shall be saved. Mohammed, Buddha, Confucius don't even come close to Him.

Paul said of Jesus in Philippians 2:9 God has highly exalted His Son and giving Jesus a Name above every Name. One day Mohammed, Buddha, and Confucius will bow before that Name above every Name.

Paul the Apostle is unambiguous when it comes to this in verses 10 and 11. Every knee will bow; every tongue will confess that Jesus Christ is Lord to the Father's Glory. You will bow to Him one day whether you like it or not.

Satan will one day bow to Him; every Atheist will bow to Him. I would rather bow to Him now than bow to Him later. At the Great White Throne at history's end, Jesus will be Judge, jury, and executioner.

At the Great White Throne all the unsaved dead will be summoned out of hell where they are now and stand before Jesus. The books (plural) are open, containing the record of their deeds from the womb to the tomb.

Then, a Book, (singular) is open, the Book of Life. That Book contains the names of the redeemed. The names of the unsaved dead are not in that one book. Based on that, they are cast into the lake of fire.

Jesus can be your Savior now, or your Judge later. You can bow to Him now, or, bow to Him later. What will you do with that Name which is above every Name. Jesus is coming soon, and the earth is ripe for God's judgment. The Rapture is so close at hand.

Notes

Wise Men Still Seek the Jewish Messiah Today

Matthew 2: 1-6

1 Now when Jesus was born in Bethlehem of Judaea in the days of Herod the king, behold, there came wise men from the east to Jerusalem,

2 Saying, Where is he that is born King of the Jews? for we have seen his star in the east, and are come to worship him.

3 When Herod the king had heard [these things], he was troubled, and all Jerusalem with him.

4 And when he had gathered all the chief priests and scribes of the people together, he demanded of them where Christ should be born.

5 And they said unto him, In Bethlehem of Judaea: for thus it is written by the prophet,

6 And thou Bethlehem, [in] the land of Juda, art not the least among the princes of Juda: for out of thee shall come a Governor, that shall rule my people Israel.

Even some 2,000 years later after the events in Matthew 2, Wise men still seek the Messiah, the Son of God, Yeshua HaMachiach. Wise men still seek Him for salvation because Yeshua is the only way to Salvation.

Remember, Salvation in Hebrew is Yeshua, Yeshua is the first century birth Name of Jesus. Jesus is a Jew, born in the little Jewish town five miles south of Yerushalyim, (Jerusalem). He was from the tribe of Judah. Jesus is the Lion of the tribe of Judah. We say, Yehudah in Hebrew. Leadership comes from the tribe of Judah.

The word "Judah" is where we get the term "Jew" from. Abraham was called a Hebrew in Genesis 14:13, Jacob's name was changed to Israel, Genesis 32:28, and Judah was called the first Jew in 2 Kings 16:6.

Yaacov, Jacob gave a prophecy concerning his 12 sons in Genesis 49:10 that the Messiah would come from the tribe of Judah, Judah would be Royalty and be the head of all the other tribes. Shilo comes from Judah.

We say "Sheelo" in Israel, not Shilo (Shyloah) as we pronounce it here in the West. The Rabbis tell us that Shilo is another Name for the Messiah. Messiah comes from Judah, Judah is where we get the word Jew from.

In Judges 1:2 Judah leads the charge against the Canaanites, "Judah shall go up". In Revelation 7:4 describing the 144,000, 12, 000 each from the 12 tribes of Israel, Judah is first mentioned in that list.

We see in Hebrews 7:14 the writer of that book describes our Lord coming from the tribe of Judah. And, we see in Revelation 5:5 that Yeshua at His second coming will come as the Lion of the tribe of Judah.

The Lion of Judah, in Hebrew "Ariah Yehudah". When on the cross the Messiah spilled His blood for all mankind, the inscription read, "King of the Jews". In Hebrew "Melech Ha, Yehudim". He came as a Lamb led to the slaughter. He will return as the conquering Lion, the King of kings, in Hebrew, Melech Ha,Melechim".

We find the Messianic story in Matthew. His name in Hebrew is "Matteaoo", a Jewish Publican, or Tax collector which at that time was very unpopular.

Matthew records the story of the Wise Men who came from the east to seek the new born King. They are called Magi, they studied the stars, they were stargazers. Herod was ruler in Judea at this time from 37 to 4 B.C.

Herod was the son of Antiparter, an Edomite who became king by Roman decree around 47 B.C. These Magi probably came over from both Persia and Babylon and were experts in Astronomy.

The Bible does not tell us how many Wise Men there were, the Bible just simply says "Wise Men". We get the traditional number, 3 Wise Men because of the three gifts of Gold, Frankincense, and Myrrh. That does not prove three men.

These Wise men first set their sights on Jerusalem, why? That's the holy city of God. This infant King surely must be born in the capitol of the Jews, the holy city of God, the seat of Jewish leadership.

Herod wanted to know where this child will be born. The Wise men and Herod probably did not have a Scriptural knowledge of Messianic prophecy. They possibly had no Bible knowledge to know where the Messiah would be born, (Matt 2:2-4).

Herod now confronts the Jewish religious leadership, since they are the "experts" in the Scriptures, (I say that tongue in cheek). Herod demanded where this Messiah King would be born, show us the prophecy.

The Chief Priest, "Ha, Coomehr, Ha, Rashi", the Sanhedrin, consisting of the Parushim, the Pharisees and the Sadducees. Directed Herod's attention to Micah 5:2 concerning the location of the Messiah's birth, (Matt 2:6).

Inductive Bible study is to compare Scripture with Scripture, parallel passages. In this case Micah 5:2 is parallel with Matthew 2:6. We see the same parallel passages concerning Yeshua's birth in Isaiah 7:14 and Matthew 1:23.

In Matthew 2:7 Herod secretly called the Wise men to inquire what time the star appeared, he wanted their expert opinion since they were ancient Astronomers and studies the stars.

When they ascertained from the Scriptures where the Messiah would be born, Herod sent the Magi to Bethlehem, the House of Bread in Matthew 2:8. The Wise men possibly read the Scriptures and understood the prophecy.

They followed the Star until it led them to the location of the child, (Matt 2:9-10). The word Star in Hebrew is "Kochav", and some believe it was the actual Shekinah, the Glory of HaShem that led them to Yeshua.

When they arrived, their lives were changed forever! They saw the prophecy of Micah fulfilled before their eyes. The Scriptures are true and accurate! They presented their gifts to Him, they worshiped the Messiah King, (Matt 2:11).

In Matthew 2:12 they were warned by God not to report back to Herod and departed back to their own countries in the east. Their lives forever changed! They encountered the Creator of the Universe wrapped in human flesh as an infant.

Some 2,000 years later, wise men still seek the Son of God, their lives have been changed and transformed as did mine on April 22, 1988 at 10:49 AM at work. I experienced the Messiah who changed my life.

I received His "Metanah Cheenahmee, "Free Gift of eternal life. During Christmas we buy gifts, the greatest gift you can get is the gift of God in Romans 6:23, the gift of everlasting life.

Yeshua promised eternal life to all who come to Him by faith. Wise men still seek Him today. Jesus will one day return and call His Bride home to be with Him at the Rapture of the church!

118

Notes

The Theocratic Kingdom of The Messiah to Come

Revelation 20:2-7

2 And he laid hold on the dragon, that old serpent, which is the Devil, and Satan, and bound him a thousand years,

3 And cast him into the bottomless pit, and shut him up, and set a seal upon him, that he should deceive the nations no more, till the thousand years should be fulfilled: and after that he must be loosed a little season.

4 And I saw thrones, and they sat upon them, and judgment was given unto them: and [I saw] the souls of them that were beheaded for the witness of Jesus, and for the word of God, and which had not worshipped the beast, neither his image, neither had received [his] mark upon their foreheads, or in their hands; and they lived and reigned with Christ a thousand years.

5 But the rest of the dead lived not again until the thousand years were finished. This [is] the first resurrection.

6 Blessed and holy [is] he that hath part in the first resurrection: on such the second death hath no power, but they shall be priests of God and of Christ, and shall reign with him a thousand years.

7 And when the thousand years are expired, Satan shall be loosed out of his prison,

We have three school of thoughts concerning the doctrine that we call the Millennial Kingdom Reign of Jesus the Messiah. We believe this Kingdom is not in the present, but still future, and it will be literal.

This future Kingdom to come will be ruled by Jesus the Messiah, the Son of the living God. He will rule from Jerusalem, earth's Capitol in the Davidic Theocratic Kingdom. Jesus will reign from David's Throne.

This Kingdom will last for 1000 years. We find six times in Revelation 20:2-7 the phrase, "Thousand Years". Are we to take this literally? Or, figuratively? I believe it should be taken as a literal bodily reign.

There is no rhyme or reason whatsoever to allegorize this passage of Scripture and say it means something else. The Scripture itself gives no justification at all, nor the allowance to say we should take this allegorically.

Six times, the Bible uses the phrase, *"Thousand Years"*. If God said it once, that's good enough for me, but when He says it six times, we need to listen up! We must take this as a literal thousand years. There is no reason to see it otherwise.

The differing views concerning the Millennial Kingdom are: Pre-Millennial, Jesus returns before the inauguration of the Kingdom, Post-Millennial, Jesus returns at the end of the 1000 years, A-Millennial, there is no literal Kingdom. The latter is the major dominant view in the church today unfortunately.

We hold to the Pre-Millennial position. Jesus will return at the end of the tribulation prior to the establishment of the Kingdom. When He establishes the Kingdom, there will be 1000 years of peace.

That is not the case now, which poses a problem for the Dominion Now advocates who pontificate that we are living in the Kingdom in the present. If we are living in the Kingdom now I'm sorry I signed up for this deal!

The Dominion Now or Kingdom Now camp teaches that Jesus is reining over the nations in the present. If Jesus is ruling over the nations in the present tense, then He is doing a poor job of doing so.

The present condition now and the biblical conditions of the Millennial Kingdom simply don't add up at all. The Millennium is a time of bliss, harmony among nations and the animal kingdom, no wars or corruption.

Question, is that the case now? No! Obviously, that is not the case now because you have wars, you have a carnivorous animal kingdom tearing each other up, you have corruption at all levels, sin abounds.

Based on Isaiah 2:2-3 and Micah 4:3-4, when Jesus is reigning, all wars are suppressed, and the nations are subjugated. There is no room in the Theocratic Kingdom of Messiah for wars and Government corruption,

2 And it shall come to pass in the last days, [that] the mountain of the LORD'S house shall be established in the top of the mountains, and shall be exalted above the hills; and all nations shall flow unto it.

3 And many people shall go and say, Come ye, and let us go up to the mountain of the LORD, to the house of the God of Jacob; and he will teach us of his ways, and we will walk in his paths: for out of Zion shall go forth the law, and the word of the LORD from Jerusalem.

4 And he shall judge among the nations, and shall rebuke many people: and they shall beat their swords into plowshares, and their spears into pruninghooks: nation shall not lift up sword against nation, neither shall they learn war any more.

Are these the conditions in the present now? Obviously not! These are future conditions of the Kingdom, not the here and now. So, Kingdom Now Theology is a fallacy doctrine with no biblical support.

If we are in the Kingdom in the present, the animal kingdom would be in harmony. They would not be trying to eat each other now. Kids would handle venomous snakes, animals would be herbivorous, not carnivorous,

Isaiah 11:6-9

6 The wolf also shall dwell with the lamb, and the leopard shall lie down with the kid; and the calf and the young lion and the fatling together; and a little child shall lead them.

7 And the cow and the bear shall feed; their young ones shall lie down together: and the lion shall eat straw like the ox.

8 And the sucking child shall play on the hole of the asp, and the weaned child shall put his hand on the cockatrice' den.

9 They shall not hurt nor destroy in all my holy mountain: for the earth shall be full of the knowledge of the LORD, as the waters cover the sea.

Why do we use the term "Millennium"? Many in the church object to the use of the word. They also object to the use of the word, "Rapture". They say both words don't appear in the Bible and that's true.

The word "Millennium" comes from two Latin words, 'Mille' (Thousand), 'annum", (years), thus, one thousand years. The word Rapture comes from Latin word *"caught up"* in 1 Thessalonians 4:17, as *Raptura*, which means to seize or snatch away.

All because a word doesn't appear in the Bible does not mean the doctrine isn't there. We use the words Trinity, Rapture, Millennium, Missions, Missionary, and the word, Bible. These words don't appear in the Bible, but the doctrine connected to these words are there.

In the Kingdom to come Jesus will reign from Jerusalem, the center of the earth, (Ezek 5:5). He will re-establish David's Throne and sit on that Throne, (2 Sam 7:16; Isa 9:6-7; Luke 1:32-33). Jerusalem will be the Throne of the Lord, (Jer 3:17).

Jesus Himself will build a fourth Temple (Zech 6:12-13), the Millennial Temple described by Ezekiel in chapters 40-46 covering 202 detailed verses about the Messiah's Temple in the Davidic Kingdom.

Jesus will reign through three classes of Kingdom Administrators, the Apostles and the church, (Matt 19:28-29), the Old Testament Saints who are resurrected at this time, (Isa 26:19; Dan 12:2), and, the Tribulation Saint martyrs, (Lk 19:12-27; Rev 20:4).

There was a Theocracy in the past, a Satanocracy in the present, and in the future, a Theocracy will once again be re-established. A Theocracy is the rule of God and the nations subjugated to that rule, that is not the case now.

Between Genesis 1-2 there was a Theocracy, with the fall of man in Genesis 3 to Revelation 19 there is a present Satanocracy, from Revelation 19 to Revelation 22, a Theocracy will be re-established. Jesus is King.

The Kingdom is not now, but future, (Matt 6:10). The Kingdom will be literal, and Jesus will reign bodily. Before the Kingdom, before the second coming, before the tribulation, the Rapture is the next event!

Final Thoughts

It is my prayer that this book will reinforce your belief that the Rapture is a biblical doctrine and one we can take hope and comfort in. If we study the Scriptures and interpret it correctly from a plain sense interpretation, you will see that doctrine fits like a hand in a glove. We must avoid the hype and drama associated with some prophecy teachers today and look to the Scriptures for our doctrine.

We must be in a local Bible believing gospel preaching church where God's Word is honored and a passion for souls being won. We see apostacy and liberal elements permeating the church at an alarming rate. Christians are falling for every wind of doctrine under the sun and failing to get their doctrine from personal study of the Bible.

We spoke about doctrinal truths in this book. We looked at the Bible from a plain sense interpretation. There is no hype, no drama, or sensationalism at all in this Eschatological study. My goal for this book was to defend the truth of the doctrine of the Rapture. The blessed hope of the Rapture is biblical, Jesus promised He would return for His church.

Global conditions are showing we are at the edge of eternity. Jesus is about to step out of heaven with a shout! A shout! Of the Archangel, and the blowing of a shofar, that is Hebrew for trumpet, or Ram's horn. When the trumpet sounds the dead in Christ, from Pentecost until now, all the born-again dead shall rise from the graves. Then, we who are alive at the Rapture will meet the Lord in the air.

What a glorious event that will be! The Rapture of the church is the hope of all believers and followers and Jesus. This world is not our final home. We are pilgrims passing through. We are strangers in this world. This world hates us because of who we follow. They hated Jesus before they hated us. They crucified our Lord because He preached absolute truth. The world hates us today because we preach that same absolute truth.

Are You Saved?

If you're not saved I would love to show you how to be saved. It's as simple as A. B.C. God loves you and wants to see you in heaven someday. God created us with free will to either accept or reject His Son.

A. All have sinned and come short of the glory of God, (Rom 3:23)

B. Believe on the Lord Jesus Christ and thou shalt be saved, (Rom 10:13)

C. Confess your sins to the Lord and ask Jesus to forgive you of all your sins, (Rom 10:9-10).

God has a gift for you, the gift of eternal life, (Rom 6:23). How do you receive that gift? By faith! Ask the Lord to come into your heart and be your Savior. It's either heaven or hell depending on what you do with Jesus now. Pray something like this:

Lord Jesus, forgive me of my sins. I deserve your wrath and judgment, but I fall on your mercy and ask you to save me from my sins. I receive your free gift of eternal life. Help me to live my life for you. I want to be ready for either death, or the Rapture. Thank you, Jesus, in your Name I pray, amen.

Welcome to the family of God! You are ready for either one or two events, death or the Rapture. It's a win, win, situation either way as a child of God. We are on the winning side. Share your faith with others. Find a Bible believing church to fellowship and grow. Read your Bible daily. Be in prayer consistently. And let's pray *MARANATHA*! Even so come Lord Jesus!

Notes

Notes

Notes

Notes

Notes

Notes

Notes